The Duck Who Watched

How Ordinary Homes and Everyday Habits Quietly Shorten Our Lives

Marko Vovk

Paperback: ISBN: 978-1-969955-29-7

E-Book: ISBN: 978-1-969955-31-0

Cover design: Marko Vovk (Draft 1, February 2nd 2026) Interior design: Marko Vovk

Final editing by Marko Vovk (some minor inconsistencies may remain; no outside paid editor was used).

Printed in the United States of America.

Portions of this material are adapted from Marko Vovk's books Fix Your Toxic Home and Live Longer, The Sixth Extinction, and other thoroughly researched nonfiction works, together with insights drawn from more than 18,000 home inspections over the last 45 years.

Contents

Chapter One

Chapter 1 – Lady in Her Easter Dress

Spring clung to the street like a secret almost ready to break loose. Cool air settled over the damp sidewalk and dark patches. A small pile of dirty snow hunched in the gutter, streaked with grit and leaves, shrinking by the hour. The morning felt new, but not unfamiliar.

Lady Weatherwaddle stood at the top of the duplex steps in her Easter outfit. Her pastel dress fell in a careful line to the step. A matching bonnet hugged her round head, its bow fixed under her beak. Her paint had been touched up and worn again so often that the colors no longer quite matched.

She had stood on this porch for almost twenty years now, in one costume after another. Winters and heat waves had moved through this block. New roofs went on, and peeled paint flaked away. Cars came and left, families too. The street changed its surface. Its habits stayed.

Back in the mid-1980s, ducks and geese like her had appeared on porches all over the neighborhood. They wore raincoats, graduation gowns, Halloween capes, and red-white-blue stripes. Some had painted eyelashes or tiny wooden glasses. For a while, neighbors quietly competed through their ducks' outfits.

Most of those birds were gone now, carried inside or hauled away. This one remained.

Today she wore her Easter dress again: soft pastel with a scalloped hem and bonnet ribbon tied under her beak. The gray porch boards beneath her showed old wood at the edges, dark and hard from years of footsteps. Tiny cracks caught dust that never quite left.

Behind her, the two-family house rose in a square, practical block. Two mailboxes sat side by side beside the front door. A thickly painted rail ran along the steps, ridges frozen in place from long-ago jobs. The porch held just enough space for the duck, two clay pots waiting for geraniums, and a metal chair no one used much anymore.

Above, the second-floor window watched the street through glass and clutter. Porcelain figures crowded the sill. Small framed photos leaned against the pane. A crooked vase held a plastic flower. Yellowed curtains pulled back with ribbons that matched nothing else.

The window belonged to the upstairs widow. She had been quicker once, lifting the duck and swapping outfits in a single, practiced sweep. Now she moved more slowly, but still kept everything.

The upstairs door creaked open.

"Hold still," she murmured, as if the duck might step away. Her slippers whispered over the porch boards. Her housecoat hung colorless, but her hands adjusted the bonnet ribbon with sharp, practiced fingers.

She coughed once, a dry, scraping sound that seemed to start deep. Dust shimmered in a shaft of hallway light behind her. The air carried a faint mix of old perfume, stale smoke long soaked into fabric, and the chalky scent of stored things.

"I should dust more," she said, half to herself. "Or open that window."

Her eyes flicked toward the living room behind her. Through the open door, stacks and shelves showed themselves in a quick, cluttered slice. Holiday bins with handwritten labels. Overfull bookcases bending in the middle. Boxes of fabric and craft supplies. A sewing machine on a small table, thread still strung. A laundry basket full of folded duck costumes for every season.

She patted the bonnet once more.

"There," she said. "Ready for spring."

Letting go of anything in that room would have meant admitting some "someday" might never come. Holding on meant moving through dusty air and coughing more each week. For her, the second weight felt lighter than the first.

The door clicked shut. The street claimed the porch again.

Below, the downstairs door snapped open with a jangle of keys.

The renter spilled out in a rush. A black North Face hoodie hung half-zipped over a worn T-shirt. A red Ohio State cap sat low on his forehead, brim bent just so. Reebok shoes squeaked against the threshold, bright logo flashing as he stumbled forward with a travel mug and bag.

"No, I'm already late," he said into the phone pinned between cheek and shoulder. "I'm leaving right now."

His laptop bag bulged with folders and cables. Yesterday's mail stuck out of a side pocket. Keycards and a gym fob dangled from his belt. The travel mug steamed in his hand, lid sealed tight.

He fought with the lock while still talking.

"Yeah, I'll call them. If the email bounced, I'll resend it from the office. Just give me a second."

The keys snagged on the metal faceplate. Coffee sloshed close to the brim. He muttered something sharp under his breath and twisted harder.

For a moment, the door swung wider, revealing the entryway behind him. Shoes had accumulated near the mat, scattered in a pile. A delivery box sat half-opened, plastic packing spilling out. Flyers and envelopes leaned in a slant on a small table. A logo-heavy jacket lay tossed over the back of a chair already holding two other layers.

North Face, Reebok, Ohio State, three streaming subscriptions, a new phone, and an older car. The brands and bills changed, but the stacks at the door always looked the same.

He kicked the door closed with a practiced thud.

"Look, I'm in the car in two minutes," he said. "Traffic willing, I'll be there in twenty. I didn't forget; I just—yeah. Okay."

He jogged down the steps. The travel mug left a faint ring where it had rested on the rail for a heartbeat. Keys rattled, laces trailed, hoodie flapped as he headed to the street.

His car idled at the curb, exhaust curling white in the cool air. He dove in, tossed the bag on the passenger seat, and pulled away with a jerk. The front wheel clipped the edge of a cracked storm drain cover, rattling it in its frame.

The space he left behind looked larger for a moment, then smaller again. From this porch, it had always looked like that. Twenty years of rushing figures, piles of packages, and branded clothes, leaving at a sprint, then coming back just as tired.

Her painted eyes sat wide and to the sides, giving her a broad view up and down the block. She saw every stoop across the street and the pieces of the houses at each end. Colors came through sharply: the flash of a red ball, the blue of recycling bins, the faded green of a plastic frog in a garden bed. Motion pricked at the edge of her sight: curtains shifting, a hand lifting in a half-wave, a front wheel spinning when a bike tipped over.

Some things stayed out of direct view. The side houses lived mostly in hints. One offered only a driveway and glimpses of bumpers. The other showed trash cans and the edge of a fence. Their habits reached her through sound and smell. She heard the hum of a vacuum on schedule, overlapping barks and meows, and the clank of glass in bins. Bleach bit the air on hot days. Arguments rose and faded after midnight.

Across the street, the four leading houses woke in their usual ways.

The first yard belonged to what she thought of as the volleyball family. A crooked net leaned against the garage, its cords knotted. A ball rested half-deflated near the fence, dusted with sand that never quite washed off. A plastic trophy, gold paint flaking, sat forgotten on a low wall near the porch. The whole yard looked as if a team had rushed in and never really unpacked.

Their minivan sat low in the drive, tired and crowded. Dull paint told of years of hands and backpacks. The rear window held ghost shapes of old stickers. Through the glass, the back seat showed a soccer ball and two booster seats. A forgotten sweatshirt lay beside a crumpled fast-food bag rolled tight.

Lady had watched one of their kids grow up on that stretch of concrete. Four long years of travel weekends and late returns, sand shaking off shoes at midnight, duffel bags dropped on the porch. The girl had left for college to study something in hospitals, a degree with promise. Now, a slightly older version occasionally reappeared in a different car, bringing laundry and worries back home.

Next door, the young couple's house felt like the citrus-clean house. The porch stood neat and balanced, two matching pots flanking the door. The soil there was always dark and damp, never left dry for long. A welcome mat lay perfectly straight, its letters only lightly worn.

A faint scent drifted from the doorway: citrus cleaner, fresh laundry, and a floral plug-in. A dog toy, a rubber ring with minor tooth marks, rested near the top step. Inside, a medium dog with a white eye patch pressed its paws against the sill. Each breath fogged the window. The glass clouded and cleared in a steady rhythm.

Third in line stood the dog-walking, late-TV house. Blinds hung half-drawn, letting a strip of light cross the couch inside. The television glowed even in the early morning, screen blue and restless. A cat sat in the front window, tail wrapped around its paws, watching a bird hop across the yard. The recycling bin overflowed with flattened boxes, labels from food delivery, and other people's pet supplies.

The single neighbor who lived there often walked past this block, handles of leashes looped in both hands. Some days, two dogs. Some days three or four, none the same. The walks started at odd hours, sometimes before dawn, sometimes near midnight, but the TV light often stayed on behind him, a backdrop that never quite turned off.

At the far end, the lawn-ornament house sat slightly slumped but busy. The siding had faded. The trim's crisp lines had softened into rounded edges. Metal flowers spun crookedly in the breeze. A smiling sun on a stake showed a crack cutting through one painted eye. A wind chime clinked lazily. On weekends and many weekdays, an older man pushed a mower across the narrow lawn or directed a leaf blower along the sidewalk. Snow disappeared from his walkway faster than from anyone else's.

Through the front window, a daytime TV show flickered over two shapes instead of one. One belonged to him. The other, frailer silhouette in a chair or wheelchair, belonged to his elderly mother. Money came on the first of the month. Gas went into the car most afternoons, sending it toward the highway. The porch watcher could not see the casino, but she could tell the pattern of the trips by time and weight.

Another house further down the block never seemed to settle. Cars rotated through its drive: small, then large, old, then new. Porch furniture appeared and vanished—iron, plastic, then bare concrete. Curtains changed styles often. For a few months, bright cushions appeared. Then they vanished again. The house tried on lives like outfits, never keeping one long.

A different side house identified itself by its smells. On breezy mornings, sharp lemon and pine scents rolled across the street. The vacuum's whine marched back and forth every Saturday. Now and then, the glass flashed as a cloth hung on the windows.

On the opposite side, the pet-heavy house announced itself through sound and weight. Dogs barked in staggered pitches until a voice snapped them quiet. Cats yowled at unseen rivals. On collection days, cans there groaned under heavy loads of food tins, litter, and chewed plastic.

Few people ever spoke directly to the duck. To most, she blended into the railing and pots, part of the porch, not a witness. She watched anyway.

A wet ripping sound suddenly tore through the morning.

At the volleyball family's house, the front door banged open. One parent hauled a swollen black garbage bag across the porch, plastic stretched tight and thin. They heaved it toward the curb. Halfway down the walk, the bottom seam split.

The contents spilled out in a slow, ugly wave. Crumpled takeout boxes tumbled onto the concrete, lids still greasy. Glossy mailers exploded in a paper fan. A plastic banner and unused decorations slid free, still sealed. Juice boxes rolled under the hedge, straws unpierced. A small toy in a clear package skidded across the sidewalk, untouched since purchase.

The air puffed with a sweet, sour smell. Spoiled leftovers and rotted fruit had forgotten their purpose in the back of the fridge. A crushed cupcake landed frosting-side down, icing smearing in a neon streak across the gray.

"Come on," the parent muttered. They glanced up and down the street, cheeks flushing. No one looked back. Only the porch watcher's painted eyes stayed fixed.

They tore a fresh bag from a roll tucked under one arm. Knees creaked as they crouched. Handfuls of trash moved from cracked plastic to new plastic. The unopened toy paused in their grip.

"I don't even remember buying this," they said quietly.

For a beat, it looked like they might set it aside. The child inside yelled from somewhere deeper in the house.

"Mom! Where's my jersey?"

The parent flinched. The toy dropped into the new bag with a small thump.

"There," they said. "Just cleaning up."

They knotted the top tight enough that the plastic squealed. Both bags were dragged to the curb. The torn one got wadded and shoved on top of the whole load.

The watcher did not wrinkle an absent beak at the smell. She had seen worse splits in summer heat. Raccoons would find this pile later. Wind would chase stray wrappers down the street. The money inside those bags had turned to trash long before the seams split.

A sedan pulled up in front of the volleyball house while the parents still stood at the curb—the engine cut. A young woman stepped out, shoulders squared but eyes tired.

She moved with traces of her younger self, a slight hop when she fixed her shoe. Glance at the upstairs window, as if expecting someone to wave. The porch steps made her straighten, as if bracing for old rules.

The watcher remembered her smaller. This driveway had once held a different car. A child version of this woman had jumped from its back seat, volleyball bag thumping, hair in a crooked ponytail. She had left chalk drawings on the sidewalk and stickers on the mailbox. Weekends used to mix sand from tournaments into the porch floorboards.

Now she opened the trunk and lifted out a laundry basket stuffed with clothes. A box of kitchen items followed. Another plastic bin held textbooks and a rolled-up poster from a hospital training session. The bags under her eyes no longer came from late games.

"Just for a little while," she called toward the open front door. "Until I figure the job thing out."

"You know you can always come home," someone answered from inside.

She balanced the basket against her hip and climbed the steps. Her gaze flicked once toward the new minivan, once toward the trash bags, then slid past the duck on the opposite porch.

Recognition didn't show. For the watcher, memory filled in everything the girl had forgotten.

People left this block. They came back again with different baggage. Cars aged out and got replaced. Degrees promised futures, then offered less than expected. The porch stayed put.

A bird called high above, sharp and bright. Somewhere, a dog barked and another answered. A voice snapped them quiet. The mail truck turned the corner, brakes squealing.

Upstairs, the widow's silhouette moved behind the curtain. She paused with a hand on the glass, looking down at the duck and then across the street. Her breath clouded the pane briefly before she turned back into her crowded, coughing house.

Lady Weatherwaddle stood in her Easter dress, bonnet ribbon firm under her beak, while another spring morning unfolded in its familiar way. Rushing. Cleaning. Tossing. Buying. Leaving. Returning.

The seasons on this street kept changing their costumes. Snow melted into rain, then into grass. Heat-baked sidewalks before leaves dropped and frost returned. People changed their cars, their jobs, their logos, and sometimes their addresses.

Now, most weeks, only one or two households sent anyone on foot. A pair from the duplex at the corner might appear, walking with small steps and in careful clothes. Sometimes it was the sharp-suited man from the bigger house, keys in hand and face already set for the day. They usually left and returned in under an hour, as if faith itself had been squeezed into a tight appointment.

The rest of the block stayed in pajamas and T-shirts. Screens glowed behind their curtains while the bell still rang outside. Some shuffled to the kitchen for coffee and scrolled with one eye on the clock.
From the porch, it

The way they spent their days changed much more slowly, if at all. Time is still in a hurry. Money still fed bags that split at the curb.

Sunlight climbed the fronts of the houses. Toys, trash, trophies, ornaments, and porch boxes brightened one by one. From the porch where she stood, it looked like another brand-new season.

A few days after that garbage split at the curb, the upstairs widow eased her way down the porch steps, one hand firm on the rail. She had dressed the duck that morning in a plainer spring dress, light green with tiny painted flowers brushed along the hem and a fresh ribbon at the neck.

It was not as fancy as the Easter outfit, just an everyday "busy season" dress for a block that never really slowed down. She straightened the bow with two quick fingers, then stood a moment watching the minivan across the street before turning back inside.

Chapter Two

Chapter 2 - "The New Minivan."

From the same porch, it looked exactly like the others.

Morning hit the family house like a switch. Doors slammed. Kids shouted over each other. Backpacks dropped in a bright, chaotic heap on the steps. The noise shoved the day into motion.

In the drive, the old minivan sagged under its usual load. Dings pocked the doors like old bruises. A long scrape chewed along the rear bumper. Some dents came from delivery cars backing out too fast from across the street, hitting and running without a note.

Inside, the floor held the shapes of forgotten cups and crushed wrappers. Grease stains marked where bags had leaked. Fries and crumbs made a thin carpet under the seats. The air carried that stale mix of salt, sugar, and old soda.

Concrete around it already looked crowded. Sports gear leaned against the garage wall in a lopsided pile. Scooters sprawled sideways, not the old foot-push kind, but heavy electric ones. The kids who rode them were heavier too, padded by constant snacks and meals from boxes and bags.

On garbage days, their cans sagged at the curb: empty cereal boxes, plastic bottles, and frozen-meal trays pressed against the lids. Bright cartoon mascots grinned from crumpled cardboard, promising energy and fun. From across the street, it looked like most of the family's food lived in packages and was poured from bags.

The same brands that filled their cans filled their bodies, one quick bite at a time. Labels talked about vitamins. The ingredients list told a longer, smaller story in tiny print.

The front door jerked open. Two adults stepped out mid-argument.

"We can't keep driving this thing," one said, flicking a hand at the minivan. "It's not safe with them in the back."

"It runs," the other answered. "We just did the brakes."

"Mostly isn't good enough," the first said. "We need safer. Bigger. Reliable."

"Safer" carried more weight than anything else. The kids heard "bigger" and "new." That was enough.

"Are we getting a new car?" one child shouted, bouncing. He wanted a Jeep like his friends at school, with rubber ducks on the dashboard. The car you stepped out of meant more than what was in your head.

"Does it have screens in the back?" another asked. "And cup holders? Real ones, not the sticky kind."

Those features sounded less like extras and more like survival gear. The kids listed them with the urgency of oxygen. They knew model names better than book titles.

Across the street, the porch watcher took in the scene. Years earlier, a boxy station wagon had filled that exact spot. Before that, a compact car had crouched there like a patient animal. Everyone arrived with similar promises and left the same way: dusty, dented, crumb-filled.

The family started loading into the old van for one last important trip. A sliding door shrieked along its track. A buckle snapped with a sharp click. One kid argued over who got "the good side." Another complained the belt felt too tight.

"Everyone in," one adult ordered. "We're going to look, not buy."

"Sure," the other said. "We always say that."

The engine coughed, caught, and settled into a tired idle. Exhaust drifted up in a gray ribbon. The van pulled away with a wobble that made the driver wince and grip the wheel harder. Faded bumper stickers clung to the back window, ghosts of old seasons and causes.

The space they left behind looked naked. Tire ghosts striped the pavement. A clean rectangle of concrete showed where the sun had not reached for months. Without the vehicle, the clutter around it jumped into focus: balls rolling, bikes leaning into the space.

The drive itself showed cracks and patches, lines of old caulk, and sinking slabs. Big repairs cost more than they had left after bills, sports, and trips. Patching, not replacing, had become part of this family's language.

Time slid past in small street motions. An Amazon truck pulled up instead of the old mail van, doors slamming, boxes thumping onto porches. A dog-walker passed, dragged by three leashes. More dog-walkers and a few joggers followed from other blocks, circling the same few streets.

Twenty years ago, the porch watcher had seen three kids for every dog. Now it often looked the other way around. Human time and money circled leashes as much as playgrounds.

On garbage mornings, a Ford F-150 rumbled slowly down the block. It's usually a bed that carries someone else's couch, broken dresser, or old washer. The driver's eyes swept the curbs for "good trash," ready to rescue, resell, or scrap whatever the cans could not swallow. He came every week, as faithful as the collection trucks.

A plastic bag rattled along the curb like a loose ghost and snagged on a drain. It fluttered there, caught between water and road.

The watcher remembered another spring morning. A different family had climbed into a different car with the same bright tension. They had come back grinning beside a new vehicle, certain life would turn smoother with fresh paint and a warranty.

Cars kept changing. That feeling did not.

Late afternoon light stretched long across the pavement when the old minivan returned. It pulled in slowly and stopped with last-day heaviness. The engine cut off. For a moment, nobody moved.

Then the new one arrived.

It was a more expensive model, a hybrid with every bell and whistle. Payments would stretch longer than some childhoods. The shiny van rolled into view behind the old one like an upgraded shadow. Paint caught the sky and threw it back.

Reflections of houses and trees slid across the curved sides. Headlights looked clear and sharp, like alert eyes. Even standing still, the vehicle seemed to glow with promise.

Kids spilled out, shouldering past one another to reach it first. Doors slid with a soft, expensive sigh. Buttons lit when small fingers pressed them. The horn chirped once when someone hit the wrong control.

"Look, it opens by itself!" one yelled, riding the sliding door like a carnival ride.

"This seat has a charger," another crowed. "And cup holders that aren't sticky."

The adults stood near the hood, their voices raised with excitement.

"We got a good deal," one said. "They knocked off more than I expected."

The watcher knew prices always had room to "knock off." Deals moved numbers around. Payments still came every month.

"Top safety rating," the other replied. "Backup camera, lane warnings, all of it. This will make everything easier."

For a heartbeat, the vehicle almost looked holy there, an altar to fresh starts. Then they opened the old minivan like a fossil.

Layers of family life spilled into view. Sports gear clogged the rear: cleats, shin guards, deflated balls, tangled nets. Reusable bags sagged with something forgotten. Snack wrappers clung to the carpet in an uneven skin.

Crushed cups hid under seats. Crumpled worksheets stuck to the floor by some dry, unidentifiable spill. A single shoe waited in the far corner, its partner missing for months. Warm, stale air carried the smell of old food.

"Don't drag garbage into the new car," one adult warned. "Throw it out first."

They started sorting right there on the concrete. A small pile formed for "definitely garbage." Another, just as significant, was formed for "just in case." The line between them kept blurring.

Sports gear moved into the new trunk without question. So did reusable bags and emergency hoodies. Crumpled paperwork slid into seat-back pockets "for later." Half-empty bottles got tested with a quick shake. Some went into the bin. Others, judged "fine," dropped into spotless cup holders.

A greasy fast-food sack hovered over the can. McDonald's and Burger King wrappers crinkled at the top, logos still bright.

"We might need the napkins," someone said.

They shook out the stack, saved every napkin, and tossed the rest. Grease spots bloomed on the concrete.

From deep under a seat, a forgotten snack bag emerged. The expiration date had passed months ago. When they opened it, a sharp, stale smell jumped out. The chips inside had turned into strangely bright dust.

"Gross," a child said, backing away.

"Don't smell it. Just toss it," came the reply.

Bag and dust hit the bottom of the can with a soft hiss. That money had already turned to waste in the dark, long before this clean-out.

Near the back, a sports item slid into view: a pristine bat or racket, still wrapped, price tag dangling. It glowed with the promise of a season that had never happened.

They moved the old van into the garage, nose-to-nose with a rusted 1972 Cutlass that had waited there for years. That car had once been a dream project, "someday" restoration, father-child weekends with wrenches. Time and money never lined up. Dust and rust took over instead.

"I thought you needed this last season," one adult said, turning the wrapped gear.

The child shrugged. "We had the old one."

"It was on sale," the adult answered, more to themselves.

The item hovered between trunk and can, then landed on the "keep" pile. It moved to the new van, still unused, still waiting on a version of life that might never arrive.

By the time the old vehicle stood empty, the new one already carried a familiar weight. The trunk looked neat, yet crowded. Seat-back pockets bulged with papers and stray pens. Cup holders, once spotless, now held fingerprints and the first ring of condensation.

The old minivan slumped beside it. The bare interior showed every stain and worn patch. Marks on the floor told stories of constant use and hurried wipe-downs. Fabric and paint had endured years of impact, recording each one.

A neighbor walked past with their own can on wheels. They slowed when they saw the new van.

"Wow," they said. "Nice upgrade. That's a beauty. Now you're set."

A woman with dark curls wrapped in a scarf pushed a stroller past the driveway with a small boy beside her. She pointed up at a bird on the wire, Spanish sliding gently between them.

Later that week, a Black teenager from three houses over dribbled a basketball in lazy arcs along the curb, earbuds in.

He paused only long enough to let a delivery driver with an accent roll another stack of packages up the walk.

Across the street, the upstairs widow eased her way down the porch steps, one hand on the rail. She had dressed the duck that morning in a plain spring dress, light green with tiny painted flowers along the hem and a matching ribbon at the neck. It was not as fancy as Easter, just a "busy day" outfit, the kind she used when the calendar turned, but there was still too much to do to make a fuss. She straightened the bow with two quick fingers, then stood a moment watching the new van shine before turning back inside.

The watcher did not know much about that neighbor beyond the red Jeep that roared out each morning at seven-ten. Rubber ducks lined its dashboard, bouncing in a row with every bump. Long days and late returns helped keep its big payment alive.

Shoulders straightened at the praise. Smiles widened. The kids rushed to demonstrate features, pointing at the automatic doors, the ceiling vents, the screens that promised quieter drives.

No one asked whether anyone felt less rushed or less burdened. The praise landed on metal, not on the people who would ride in it.

Evening came soft and slow, but the house did not match that pace. Schedules, not sky, called the shots.

"Come on," someone yelled. "We're going to be late for practice."

Backpacks, duffels, and instruments flew into the van. Shoes thudded on concrete. One kid yelled about missing shin guards. Another shouted they were starving.

"There are snacks up front," an adult said. "Just get in."

The new engine hummed, smoother than the old cough. Headlights cut twin paths through the dim street. The backup camera glowed like a small, trusted eye.

Taillights shrank along the block, heading toward the same fields, lessons, and stores. The route had not changed. Only the shell had.

For a while, the space sat quiet. The cleaner lingered where oil had once spotted the pavement. They can now hold a fresh layer of heavy bags. Inside them lay snack dust, greasy paper, and the unused crumbs of hope.

Down the block, the mowing neighbor fired up his machine, though the grass barely brushed his shoes. He cut the same small lawn twice a week, stripes already sharp from last time. After mowing, he dragged out a hose and soaked the yard until water ran into the gutter.

Gas, water, and noise poured into that little patch so it could look the same. Fertilizer pellets glittered on the soil, waiting for rain or sprinklers to carry them toward the storm drains. From there, everything washed into the lake, a slow drip of effort and chemicals.

From this porch, the grass sometimes looked like another kind of leash. People fed it money and time so neighbors would not talk. They worked hard to keep it short and obedient, then worked again when it grew back.

The house itself showed its age in quieter ways. No additions grew from its sides, only small patches of paint over old cracks. The windows and doors stayed original; the frames were older than some of the children. Porch spindles loosened and tightened again with quick fixes as money flowed elsewhere.

Night settled over the street in layered blue. One by one, porch lights clicked on. Windows glowed with shows, homework, and late cooking. In the distance, a motion light flicked on over a garage as a raccoon shuffled past cans, hoping for an opening.

The new minivan finally returned, easing into place with a tired little bounce. Doors slid open more slowly. A wrapper dropped to the concrete and fluttered beside the tire.

One adult climbed out, shoulders sagging. The dome light caught a familiar, worn face. They pulled a bag from the backseat and rubbed at a smudge with their sleeve.

"That didn't take long," they muttered.

Inside, belts hung twisted. A plastic cup rolled when the door closed. A crumpled receipt lay on the dashboard. New-car smell already wrestled with fries and sports sweat.

On the steps, the duck in her spring dress watched the pattern lock into place.

Other vehicles had arrived shining and full of promises. All of them left someday with dents, stains, and an owner saying there still wasn't enough time. This new van would earn its scars the same way.

From across the street, it gleamed under the light, as if life had turned a corner. Yet the family's hours still poured into the same mold: driving, hurrying, juggling, cleaning, buying, throwing things away.

Fresh paint and polished glass changed quickly on this block. The way people spent their days did not.

Chapter Three

Chapter 3 – Coffee, Keycards, and the Dog

Morning snapped on at the couple's house like a harsh light. The door opened, and cool air spilled from inside. The hallway behind them glowed with early bulbs, not sunrise. The day began beneath the ceiling rather than the sky.

The dog's paws tapped against the front window in frantic little bursts. Nails ticked the glass in a steady drumbeat. Breath fogged the lower pane where its nose pressed. Yesterday's toy waited on the porch, ignored and damp from dew.

Both partners stepped out at once, already in work armor. One carried a travel mug, phone, and a laptop bag. The other juggled a different mug, a badge on a lanyard, and a tote that bulged with folders. Keycards glinted from belt loops and necks like tiny metal flags.

Behind them, the house looked still and clean. The porch did not. A food delivery sack slumped beside the recycling bin, logo bright against grease stains. A stack of empty coffee cups tilted in the bin like a cardboard tower. Another package sat on the small table, fresh tape still tight across the top.

"Did you switch your shift?" one asked, shifting their mug. "You said you might stay late."

"Depends on the call volume," the other answered. "And if that rollout breaks again. I'll text."

"Tonight's not good for cooking," the first said. "I've got that deadline."

"Tonight's never good for cooking," the second replied, with half a smile.

They laughed, but tiredness hollowed the sound.

The dog barked once, sharp and hopeful. They both flinched at the noise.

"Walk?" one called through the door, voice pitching high. "We'll do a quick loop. You'll be fine."

Leash in hand, they hustled the dog down the steps. The animal strained toward the grass, sniffing every patch like a letter from another dog. One partner checked a smartwatch, tapping the screen. The other flicked through phone notifications with a thumb.

"Come on, buddy," they urged. "We've got five minutes. Do your thing."

The dog's tail wagged faster when it tried to linger. Each pause got tugged short. The walk looked less like exploring and more like a timed drill.

At the corner, the dog dragged them toward the neighbor's tree, the one that marked the edge of the lawn-ornament house. Its lower trunk showed a ring of damaged bark, dark and rough where countless dogs had stopped and lifted a leg. What should have been clean gray wood was stained and scarred from everyone else's hurry.

The walkers all carried their little rolls of plastic bags and knotted prizes, swinging from leashes and belt loops like tiny flags. Lady imagined a future dig turning up layers of those sealed bundles, deciding this neighborhood must have worshipped its animals, each wrapped carefully in oil-based cloth and buried along the curb.

From across the street, the porch watcher saw the pattern. Even joy had been squeezed into a task, even the dog's brief break added to someone else's quiet damage.

Back on the porch, the dog panted, leash hanging slack. Someone dropped a scoop of dry food into its bowl just inside the door. The rattling kibble echoed off the tile. A water dish slid slightly, sloshing.

"We'll play later," one promised, scratching the dog's head once. "After work."

They had said that before.

On the porch table, yesterday's package claimed its throne. The logo shouted convenience and speed. Inside, something waited that had once looked like the solution to a tired evening. The box was unopened.

"We should make that meal kit tonight," one said, glancing at it. "We're wasting money."

"Tonight?" the other repeated. "I've got a late meeting. It'll be another delivery night."

"We'll cook when this quarter is over," the first answered. "Things will calm down."

"When this quarter is over," floated between them, light as steam and just as solid.

They locked the door. Keycards flashed as they clipped them to belts. The house hummed behind them, lights still burning over untouched counters.

The dog watched from the window, toy now between its paws.

"Another takeout night," one said, half under their breath.

"At least we're supporting local," the other replied.

On some weekend mornings, just after the dog-walkers thinned, a small group of four appeared at the far end of the block, Bibles tucked under their arms. Two men and two women walked in a straight line, clothes neat but not fancy, stopping every few houses to ring a bell or press a doorbell.

They always seemed to come from the same direction, toward a side street where a converted storefront now held a church logo. Over the years, Lady had noticed more curtains stayed still when they passed, more porch lights clicked quietly off.

Most people on this street ducked their heads and let the knock fade, but the four kept coming back, week after week, as if this block sat on their assigned route to save.

They cut across the small yard with quick steps. The travel mugs left tiny, dark rings on the rail where they rested for a second. Then both mugs rose again as they headed toward their cars.

A few minutes later, the first outside dog-walkers of the morning came through from other streets. One man in a neon vest let three leashes run out in a fan, small dogs trotting at different speeds, plastic bags knotted to the handles and bouncing with each step.

Behind him, two men walked side by side, three larger dogs between them, their haircuts sharp, their shirts fitted and bright against the dull sidewalk. They moved like a practiced team, trading leashes and coffee cups without speaking, the dogs weaving and untangling around their legs.

In the distance, a freight train groaned along the tracks, metal on metal grinding through the morning. Overhead, a jet climbed from the airport, sound swelling and fading as it turned. This block had learned to talk over rumbles and roars. Noise lived here the way trees once had.

When the cars pulled away, the house dropped into a version of silence. It was not very quiet. Machines kept breathing.

Inside, the fridge motor hummed. A dishwasher clicked and swished from a late start. A dryer turned with slow, heavy thumps, clothes pressing against metal. A scented plug-in whispered fake lemon into the air, layered over the sharp bite of chemical cleaners drying on counters and floors.

This was the citrus-clean house. Its windows often showed a neat interior, wiped and scrubbed. Under that shine, sprays, wipes, and plug-ins fogged the air with invisible haze. The room sparkled more from bottles than from open windows.

On Lady's porch, the duck now wore her rain-storm outfit, a slick blue coat painted to look like rubber, and a tiny yellow hat tilted over one eye. The widow had come down earlier in the week, joints stiff in the damp, to slip the coat over the spring dress and tie the hat's string under Lady's beak. She had muttered something about never trusting the forecast, even though three different weather apps glowed upstairs. The coat made the duck look ready for the weather that the humans mostly encountered through screens.

Late morning brought the first visitor of the day. A delivery driver stepped up, another box hugged to their chest. The label promised comfort, productivity, or both. They rang the bell, waited a beat, then set it down beside the first package.

The stack on the table grew taller. Cardboard edges lined up in a neat little skyline. The house kept accepting arrivals; no one had time to open.

From the window, the dog watched the retreating driver. Ears stood high. Tail thudded once, then twice. No one came to the door. The box stayed outside, absorbing sunlight.

Later, a second person arrived with keys that did not match the front door. The dog-walker. They let themselves in with practiced ease, leash already uncoiled.

"Hey, friend," they said, bending to rub soft fur. "Let's take a real walk."

For a short time, someone moved at the dog's speed. They let it sniff, linger, and pause at corners. The animal's whole body loosened, tail swinging side to side. The leash hung with a relaxed curve.

But even this walk had a schedule. The dog-walker checked their phone, glanced at the time, and turned back after a few blocks. The rhythm of their steps picked up. The last stretch became brisk again.

"See you tomorrow," they said, clipping the leash back on its hook.

Afternoon dropped more boxes on the porch. Some held gadgets to "save time." Others promised to make working from home feel like a spa. Branded tape shouted urgency even while the house's inhabitants sat miles away, racing other clocks.

The sun shifted and slid along the siding. Shadows from the packages stretched and merged with the railing. The porch table now held three boxes, then four. Each one silently claimed a future evening.

Inside, the kitchen counters stayed almost bare of food but full of products. Bottles of spray and foam are lined up along the backsplash. Wipes sat in a canister near the sink. Three scented candles stood in a row, all half-burned, all different scents.

The sink held two rinsed takeout containers, stacked but not put away. A compostable fork floated in a glass, tines warped. The room sparkled in a way that came from chemicals and purchases more than from routine.

Out on the main road, a quarter mile away, a fire station door rolled up. Sirens sometimes shrieked as trucks shot past, heading toward someone else's emergency. On certain afternoons, the low throat of engines drifted back to this quieter street. Most people barely turned their heads.

Sometimes, when the wind shifted just right, a different smell slid in. Flame-broiled burgers from the Burger King on the main strip curled through the air. The scent of char and salt reached porches long before anyone saw the sign. It was another kind of plug-in, this one for hunger and habit.

Late light shifted toward gold when the cars finally returned. Tires crunched gravel. Doors opened and closed with a heavier sound than in the morning.

One partner trudged up the steps carrying a laptop bag and a phone still lit with notifications. The other clipped a badge from their collar while juggling a paper sack and a drink carrier.

The dog exploded at the window, then at the door. Paws scrambled on the floor. Nails clicked a frantic welcome song.

"Hey, hey," one said, bending for a quick pat. "We're home. Calm down."

The greeting lasted seconds. The phone buzzed again. The laptop thumped onto the dining table and flipped open. The paper sack hit the counter with a greasy rustle.

"We said we'd use the meal kit," one reminded, eyeing the porch boxes.

"I know," the other answered. "There was no way tonight. The call ran long."

"We're basically paying to throw ingredients out," the first said.

"Next week," the second replied. "After this project, we'll start cooking."

"After this project" landed beside "when this quarter is over," a matching pair of invisible hooks.

They spread takeout cartons across the coffee table, not the dining table. Steam fogged the air for a moment, then thinned. The dog circled the edge of the room, nose lifting for every scent. Occasionally, a hand dropped a treat without looking.

The television lit the room in blue and white. A show filled the silence where conversation might have gone. Each partner ate while their eyes bounced between screen and phone.

"Promotion email went out today," one said, almost casually.

"Yours?" the other asked, pausing their fork.

"No, Mark's," came the answer. "But it means more calls, more targets. They're rolling out extra quotas."

"Of course they are," the partner said. "More for the same pay. Classic."

They ate a few more bites as the show's volume rose. A commercial promised efficiency and relaxation. The porch boxes might as well have spoken the same language.

When dinner finished, cartons slid into a plastic sack. Noodles clung to the sides. A whole side salad remained, barely touched, dressing still sealed.

"I wasn't even hungry," one said, staring at the leftovers.

"You were stressed," the other replied. "Different kind of empty."

The sack went out to the bin, where it landed with a dull, wet thud. Inside, already-forgotten dishes joined pizza boxes from earlier that week. Some containers clinked with uneaten food still inside.

In the corner of the kitchen, a small appliance sat on the counter. It had been bought to "make cooking faster." The cord snaked to the outlet, but the power light stayed dark. Dust traced a thin line along its edge.

"We should use that thing," one said, noticing it again.

"We will," the other answered. "When things slow down."

Out in the living room, the dog returned to the couch. It dropped its toy on one partner's leg and looked up, eyes bright. The partner stroked the dog's head without looking away from the screen.

"After this episode," they said. "Promise."

Episodes stacked into hours. The dog curled closer, the toy pressed between its chest and the cushion. Eyes eventually slid closed, not from contentment but from simple exhaustion.

Later, one partner tied a knot in the bulging garbage sack. It stretched around its contents like skin around a stuffed stomach. The weight made their arm drop.

On the way out, they passed the porch table. Three unopened boxes waited. One held snacks for "busy nights." Another contained a set of stylish storage containers to "control clutter." The third promised a more innovative coffee maker that could "save time every morning."

They stepped around the stack and dumped the sack into the outside can. The air filled with a flurry of mixed smells: ginger, garlic, plastic, and something sour. None of it smelled like rest.

From across the street, the duck watched the light shift in the couple's windows. The living room glowed blue, then white, then flashed with ads and scenes from other lives. The kitchen light flicked on and off in short bursts, never long enough to suggest a slow meal.

She remembered earlier years in that same house. Another couple once hurried out with different mugs, different phones, and similar bags. Before them, a single tenant came home late with takeout nearly every night. Logos changed. Patterns did not.

People here kept buying "later" in boxes, apps, and subscriptions. Later never arrived.

As night deepened, the TV volume dropped. The laptop screen still glowed faintly through a gap in the curtain. One small lamp remained on near the couch, shining over a half-finished email and an untouched self-help book.

On the floor, the dog slept curled tightly, toy under its chin. Its leash hung by the door, looped and ready, waiting for the time that kept getting spent somewhere else.

From the porch across the street, the scene looked almost peaceful. Two people, one dog, a tidy home, warm light, full bellies. That version would photograph well.

From this angle, though, it also looked like a day bought with energy they did not have. Convenience had eaten their time and then charged extra. Money had flowed out with every beep of a scanner and ping of an app. Packaging and leftovers had piled up to prove it.

On this little stretch of street, the couple's life shone like many others: bright screens, fast food, and streaming promises. The dog would get another quick walk tomorrow. The boxes would open eventually.

The keycards would still hang ready by the door.

Chapter Four

Chapter 4 – The Hobby That Never Starts

Late morning settled on the street like a lid. The rush from the family house had faded. The young couple's cars were gone. Delivery trucks had not yet started their afternoon rounds. A softer, lazier kind of noise took over.

Across the way, the single neighbor's curtains hung half open. Blue light pulsed inside from a television that never seemed to go entirely dark. Even now, with the sun high enough to touch the roofs, the screen glow still showed.

The pet in that window changed over the years. Today, it was a cat, gray with a white chin, pressed against the glass. Sometimes it was a small dog instead, ears flicking at every passing sound. Either way, something four-legged watched the world for the human who did not.

Lady Weatherwaddle had seen the same light in that window at midnight and three in the morning. Nights there never turned entirely black. Shadows in that room were shades of blue and gray, not true black. From her porch, it looked like sleep tried to live in a place that never told the brain it was night.

The cat jumped down when a truck pulled up.

A delivery vehicle eased against the curb. The driver stepped out and lifted a medium box from the back. The logo promised transformation: sleek shapes, a figure mid-stride, bright letters about "home fitness made easy."

They climbed the neighbor's steps and rang the bell. No answer. They rang again, then bent to leave the box near the door.

The lock clicked just before they turned away. The neighbor cracked the door open and squinted into the light. Pajama pants, stretched T-shirt, hair not quite brushed. Behind them, the TV mumbled to itself.

"Sorry," they said. "Didn't hear you."

They signed quickly and pulled the box inside. For a moment, the door stayed open wider than usual.

The lady could see past the entry. The hallway did not lead to open space, but to stacks. Bins of craft supplies. A guitar on a stand, a thin film of dust on its neck. A folded treadmill leaning against the wall, hangers hooked over the side, holding shirts. Shelves carried neatly lined storage cubes, each with a label fading at the edges.

Further in, a kitchen table peeked into view. Only half its surface was clear. The rest held piled mail, grocery circulars, delivery flyers, and bills spread in uncertain layers. A single plate on the edge clung to the last crumbs of a meal that had been eaten over paper.

Nothing here was dirty enough to shame. Nothing here seemed free sufficient to breathe.

The door closed. The house swallowed the box, and the light snapped back to blue.

Time dragged and then skipped. The train by the tracks moaned once. A plane from the airport rolled across the patch of sky the duck could see. A mower down the block coughed to life, then died, then roared again as the lawn-obsessed neighbor attacked his stripes for the second time that week.

He edged the grass along the walk until it formed a knife-clean line. Then he sprayed the border with weed killer, careful not to miss a seam. His yard looked like a photograph from a hardware ad. His life sounded like an engine and smelled like gasoline.

From the porch, it looked like he lived in a tiny, constant contest no one else had entered. Perfect World Syndrome, the duck thought, even if she had no name for it. Work hard to make things look flawless from the sidewalk, no matter what it costs inside.

Sometime during that stretch, the upstairs widow inched down the steps with another bundle over her arm. She swapped the raincoat for a pale yellow summer dress, sleeveless and straightforward, with small painted strawberries near the hem. The fabric had thinned from years of sun, but she smoothed it over the duck with the same care as when it was new. "Too warm for sleeves now," she said to the empty porch, breathing harder by the time she reached the top again.

Back at the single neighbor's house, movement stirred.

Midday sun had climbed higher when they reappeared at the door. They dragged the new box to the front room, shoulders rounded, slippers shuffling. The TV stayed on, volume low.

They cut the tape and folded back the flaps. Inside lay bright, promising shapes: resistance bands or sleek hand weights, a mat, maybe an app code card—the kind of gear shown on screens by people with flat stomachs and broad smiles.

They set each item out with care. The mat was unrolled on the floor between the couch and the TV. The weights are lined up under the table. They tapped their phone, pulled up a demonstration video, and watched a stranger move with easy power.

"This time," they murmured, almost to themselves. "I'll stick with it."

For a moment, their shoulders lifted. They stood a little taller. The idea of a better, stronger version of themselves seemed close enough to touch.

Then the phone buzzed with a different alert. A message popped up from a friend. The next episode in their show cued itself. A notification banner crawled across the top of the screen.

They sat back down "just to answer this." The mat waited at their feet. The new weights sat clean and ready. The video paused.

"I'll try it tonight," they said. "When I'm not so wiped."

The cat hopped onto the arm of the couch and rubbed its face against their hand. Fur brushed their fingers. They reached down, then pulled back to pick up their phone again.

Later, they carried a small plastic bag to the bins by the garage. The bag held used cat litter, knotted high. They swung it into the can without gloves, dust puffing faintly into the air before the lid clanged shut. Hands wiped quickly on pant legs, then grabbed the handle of the side door.

Inside, plug-in air fresheners blinked with tiny lights. Scented candles waited on side tables, their wicks bent. They promised "ocean breeze" and "mountain air" in a house that had neither. Cat dander floated, dog saliva dried on toys, cleaning sprays and fragrances tangled together in the rooms where this person breathed and slept.

The TV ran on.

Afternoon tilted. The sun shifted across the siding of each house. Kids' voices from the family yard rose and fell in sharp spikes. Somewhere, a basketball thumped on concrete. The red Jeep came and went, ducks on the dashboard nodding at every bump.

In the single neighbor's house, the new mat stayed smooth and unmarked. The screen showed other people moving. The person on the couch didn't.

As the day slid toward evening, they tried again.

They stepped onto the mat in socks, phone propped on the coffee table. The video instructor counted off cheerful repetitions. The neighbor copied a few movements, legs trembling after a short time. Breaths came faster, chest tight from more sitting than walking.

"This is stupid," they muttered, dropping their arms.

They looked around for space. The treadmill leaned in the corner, half storage, half guilt. A box of older hobby supplies sat on a chair, trapping it against the wall. The kitchen table still held mail and bills; there was no room for a clean plate, let alone a project.

"I need to clear this place out first," they told themselves. "Then I'll really start."

They folded the mat and slid it against the couch. The weights got tucked behind a plant stand. The phone found a show, not another workout. The pet settled near their feet, content to have company.

A commercial for lawn services played between segments. A perfect family laughed on perfect grass while a truck with a neat, uniformed logo rolled away. The neighbor watched and chewed, snack forgotten on their tongue. They already paid someone to cut the small patch out front. They wanted the benefits of movement without the sweat, the health of fresh air without stepping into it.

Taking out the trash before dark, they carried a larger bag to the curb. Crinkled packaging from the new gear rustled inside, brand names still shouting through the plastic. Flyers that had come with earlier kits slipped out and fluttered to the sidewalk.

They bent to scoop them up with a sigh.

"I really should use this stuff," they said quietly. "One of these days."

Lady had heard similar lines before from other mouths in that same doorway. Years ago, a different tenant had filled the front room with weight benches, yoga blocks, and a stationary bike hung with laundry. Before that, someone else kept art supplies and an easel, always half-turned toward a blank canvas. Hopes arrived in boxes. Effort seldom did.

Lights flicked on, one by one, as evening settled. The lawn man rolled his mower back into the shed, then brought out the hose again. Water hissed over already green blades, puddling at the curb. Fertilizer and grass bits swirled into the storm drain with a faint gurgle.

Across the street, the new minivan came and went, framing another circuit of practices and pickups. The downstairs renter stomped home in branded shoes, mail stuffed under his arm, face lit by his phone. The upstairs widow adjusted one of the duck's ribbons and coughed once, pausing to catch her breath.

Inside the single neighbor's living room, the TV volume climbed. A show became a movie, became another show. The pet curled into a ball on the couch cushion. The new hobby gear sat in a neat little cluster, already starting to look like furniture instead of tools.

Night deepened, but this house's windows never went fully dark. Blue shimmer leaked around the curtain edges, whitening the leaves of the bushes below.

The bedroom beyond that room kept a TV on low too, a faint flicker against the wall until well past midnight.

From the porch, it looked like their nights never reset. No darkness to tell the body "rest now." No silence to let the brain unclench. Just the same light and sound, a soft, constant hum of being half-awake and half-asleep.

Lady Weatherwaddle stood in her Easter dress and watched.

She had no lungs to burn with stale air, no nerves to jangle from lack of sleep. But she could see the loops people built around themselves. They bought health in boxes and then sat in front of screens. They paid others to push their mowers while their own muscles stiffened. They filled rooms with "later" and tired themselves out getting ready for changes that never came.

Cars changed. Gear changed. Even pets changed. The way many humans spent their days did not.

On this little street, the new hobby had already joined the old ones. Another someday, safely tucked where it was easy to see and easy to ignore.

Chapter Five

Chapter 5 – Vacation, on Credit

On Friday afternoon, the house spun faster.

Laundry thumped in the dryer. Someone shouted about lost shoes. A child hunted for a favorite stuffed animal. The garage door groaned open and closed as bags and coolers moved in waves.

"You don't need all those toys," a parent said, shoving a bag aside.

"You never know," came the reply. "It's only three days. Let them have fun."

They took a quick picture by the minivan, trampoline frame peeking above the fence behind them. The door of the lawn-ornament house cracked open just enough for the son to watch and take one last drag—the high-turnover rental's new tenants carried in a flat-screen.

Across the street, in the cooler morning before the heat really settled, the upstairs window brought down a brighter costume. Lady traded her soft yellow dress for a louder summer sundress, stripes of red, white, and blue running a little crooked from years of re-painting.

A tiny painted beach bag hung from one wing, seashells dabbed on in careful strokes. The widow's hands shook as she tied the ribbon, but she stepped back with a tired smile, as if sending the duck on a small vacation of her own while everyone else chased theirs on credit.

The van pulled away with a burst of sound. Horn. Shouts. A last open-window wave. Then it was gone, and the street's noise dropped a notch.

While they were away, the routine did not pause.

Flyers landed. Packages appeared. The mowing neighbor edged the grass again and soaked it until water ran down the gutter. Fertilizer pellets loosened and slid into the drain.

The retired son drove toward the casino and back, porch light off, television light on. Cigarette smoke traced faint lines up the siding. The high-- turnover rental stayed restless; new music, new cars, same small frictions with rules.

Three days later, the minivan returned. Bugs freckled the windshield. Sand dusted the mats. The kids' voices came out thinner, strained by rides, sugar, and too little sleep.

They opened the door,s and vacation spilled onto the concrete.

Souvenir cups clanked onto the porch. A stuffed animal flopped face down in the driveway. A plastic wand with dying batteries flickered half-heartedly when shaken. Half-full snack bags slumped in the back seat, air stale inside.

"I thought we'd eat those on the way," someone said.

"We were too tired," another answered. "We just grabbed whatever was there."

The parents moved more slowly now. Shoulders rounded. Eyes half-closed. One rubbed the spot between their eyebrows.

"It was worth it," they told each other. "They'll remember this forever."

The kids argued about who got to show which photo first.

A few days later, the first credit alert chimed. An envelope with a familiar logo slid through the mail slot. It landed atop two unpaid utility notices and a stack of unused coupons.

At the lawn-ornament house, the mother's window stayed dark. No one sat in the chair where she had once watched the street. Her son still left each day with the same cigarettes and the duplicate keys.

At the far rental, the new family dragged a grill onto the porch. Later that summer, someone would call the police again about noise, parking, or cans. Papers and tickets would change hands. People inside would shout. The house would keep its reputation.

On this street, addictions and habits wore different clothes. Some came in casino lights and scratchy throats. Some came in grass cut to the exact perfect length, over and over, as money and water ran off into drains. Some lived in shopping carts and on credit cards, in two-day trips bought with three months' worry.

Lady watched people feed their pets like people. They poured in time, money, and bits of health. The pets never seemed to get full.

The minivan loaded up again soon after, this time for practice, not rides. Trampoline springs complained. The mower coughed to life. The TV across the way flickered on. The duck held her spot on the porch, painted eyes wide, taking in another ordinary day that had cost more than anyone wanted to count.

Chapter Six

Chapter 6 – The Storm and the Silence

The first warning came as a chime in everyone's pocket. Phones buzzed on counters, in laps, and on porch railings. A bright banner slid across screens, telling the whole street the same thing at once: severe storm incoming.

Somewhere beyond the houses, the city sirens wound up. Their long, rising howl floated over roofs and trees. Inside, people reached for remotes. News anchors replaced game shows and dramas. Radar swirls turned red and purple across television screens, arrows and circles spinning around the city.

"Biggest storm yet this summer," one voice said. "Stay indoors. Stay away from windows."

On the family porch, a parent turned up the volume and then stood. The sky still mainly looked normal. A few more clouds. A little less blue. Nothing matched the frantic tone on the screen.

"We'd better pull the chairs in," they said.

Doors opened up and down the block. The lawn-ornament neighbor stepped out, hands on his hips, scanning his small yard as if choosing favorites. He dragged a few plastic figures closer to the house, tucked a wind spinner under the eaves, and left others standing where they were. The grass, crisp from constant cutting, lay flat as a short haircut.

The minivan family hauled in folding chairs, the camp chair that had been half open, and the loose balls scattered around the driveway. One child argued about leaving the trampoline. It was staked down and too big to move. The springs had just begun to sound like summer.

"Leave it," the parent said. "We can't take it apart in five minutes."

Across the way, the young couple shut the dog inside and pulled their porch table back toward the wall. Empty coffee cups and old delivery sacks went into the bin with hurried hands. They looked up once, then went back to checking their phones.

At the single neighbor's house, the curtains twitched. For a moment, they appeared in the window, looking from the TV to the street. Their eyes rested on the new fitness gear near the glass, then on the sky again. In the end, they closed the blinds instead of moving anything.

Light faded faster than the clock suggested it should. The sky turned from blue to flat gray to a strange, sickly green. The air grew heavy, pushing down on the street like a hand. Birds went quiet. Dogs barked once or twice and then held their tongues.

Earlier that day, before the sky had started to change, the widow had come down with yet another outfit folded over one arm. She buttoned a tiny gray cape around the duck's neck and settled a small painted umbrella into the crook of her wing, its surface dotted with blue to suggest falling drops.

The cape's paint had cracked at the shoulders where winters had bitten deepest, but she patted it flat anyway. By the time the real storm rolled over the roofs, Lady already looked as if she had been expecting it.

By late afternoon, the sky over the block had gone the color of a healing bruise—clouds stacked over the lake, thick and low.

The first gust of wind bent tree branches all in one direction. Leaves flashed their pale undersides in unison. Plastic bags, forgotten on lawns, rose and swung out into the road. Porch flags snapped stiffly, poles rattling in their brackets.

Then the rain came.

Big drops splatted onto sidewalks and driveways, dots that grew and merged. The street blurred as if someone had smeared a wet thumb across a painting. Visibility shrank until houses across the way looked like gray ghosts.

Lightning flashed, bright enough to turn the duck's shadow sharp against the house behind her. The thunder chased it almost immediately, a cracking roll that made windows buzz in their frames. Somewhere, a child shrieked and then laughed, nerves confusing fear with excitement.

Hail followed the second wave of lightning.

At first, it sounded like someone tossing handfuls of gravel onto the roofs. Small white stones bounced off shingles, thumped on car hoods, and rattled in gutters. Within seconds, it thickened. Marble--sized pellets pinged against metal railings, slapped the trampoline mat, and piled briefly in corners before the water swept them along.

Someone inside the family house cried out, "The van!" but there was no time. Stepping outside now meant getting pelted. They watched from the door instead, flinching at every louder hit.

The retired son on the ornament porch smoked faster, cigarette tip flaring in the dim. He stayed under the small overhang and watched his yard take the blows. One brittle garden ornament cracked along an old hairline fracture. He ground out the cigarette and pocketed the stub.

Then, without warning, everything else went dark.

The power cut with a sound so soft it was almost silent. No pop or bang, just a sudden absence—TV voices cut mid-sentence, fridge motors going still, fans and air conditioners sighing into nothing.

For the first time in many nights, the TV house went completely black. No blue strip at the curtain's edge. No little dots of status lights winking in the corners. The duck's eyes, fixed on that window for years, saw only storm-glossed glass.

Rain still hammered roofs and pavement. Hail thinned and then stopped, leaving only water. Thunder rumbled a little farther away now, rolling rather than cracking. In the quiet left by electricity, other sounds rose.

A baby cried somewhere down the block. A voice murmured comfort. Someone coughed a prolonged, rough cough. Another voice snapped, "We should have bought batteries," followed by the click of a useless switch.

One by one, small lights bloomed inside houses. Candles threw unsteady yellow patches against the walls. Flashlights swept across ceilings and floors, their beams weaker than their owners remembered. Phone screens glowed blue in hands, little rectangles of control.

For a minute or two, the street held absolute darkness in between those tiny flames. The sky above, streaked with lightning remnants, was darker than any TV picture. The air smelled like wet dirt, ozone, and the inside of trees.

Then the generators started.

Somewhere behind the young couple's house, a small engine coughed, sputtered, then caught. Its steady growl filled the gap left by the dead appliances. Two doors down, another machine joined in, overlapping in a low mechanical duet. A few houses glowed again, patches of steady light surrounded by candle flicker, like islands in a dim sea.

In those houses, refrigerators hummed back to life. A television screen, powered from a humming box in the yard, blinked on to show weather anchors explaining what had just happened. The rest of the block mainly stayed still.

The duck watched how quickly some people fought the silence. Darkness itself seemed like a problem to solve. Every gap had to be filled with sound, light, or information.

A sharp crack sliced through the receding thunder. It was not lightning this time. A tree, softened by water and wind, gave way at the far end of the block. Its trunk split and fell across the power lines with a grinding, snapping noise. Sparks flashed once, then died.

The outage, which might have been brief, stretched longer.

Utility trucks finally turned the corner, lights spinning in the drizzle. Workers in reflective vests stepped out, muttering as they swung up headlamps and reached for gear. For hours, they moved in and out of the beam of their own lights, arms thick with heavy gloves, voices indistinct in the distance.

Inside the houses, life shifted into a slower gear. Some families gathered in one room, candle wax dripping onto old saucers. Children complained of boredom without screens. Parents tried to turn it into a game, telling stories or playing cards with the few decks they could find.

On some porches, people sat outside again, not for chat but for air. Without fans or air-conditioning, the interior heat pushed them back onto the steps. They watched the work at the end of the street instead of the news.

The single neighbor sat in the window awhile, phone flat and screen blank, cat curled on their lap. The room looked different without the constant flicker. Dust on the shelves and the sway of the curtains drew more attention than usual.

Hours later, a collective click and whir rolled along the block. Streetlights blinked back on, one after another. Houses glowed in a staggered pattern as circuits came alive. Appliances beeped, clocks flashed, and the generators coughed themselves off.

The TV in the single neighbor's house snapped back to life almost immediately, casting its blue claim over the room again. In the young couple's house, the first move was toward the fridge and then the router. At the family house, someone groaned at the sudden brightness and reached to adjust a blinking digital clock.

Morning revealed what the storm had left.

Leaves carpeted the lawns and sidewalks in damp layers. Small branches lay scattered over driveways. Hail remnants clung in shady spots, shrinking fast in the growing heat. The tree at the end of the street lay sideways, its torn roots exposed, its crown tangled in the wires now lashed back to poles.

The minivan parents walked slowly around their vehicle. Fingers traced the hood and roof, searching for dents. A few small dimples showed in certain angles of light.

"It's not that bad," one said. "We got lucky."

Down the block, the lawn-obsessed neighbor surveyed his grass with narrowed eyes. The storm had scattered debris across his perfect stripes. He brought out the rake, then the mower, then the blower, using each as if erasing a stain. Nature's interruption became another chance to impose a pattern.

By late morning, a white van with a roofing logo rolled onto the street. Three people in matching shirts hopped out, clipboards under their arms. They moved from house to house, knocking, smiling, pointing up.

"Hail can do a lot more than you see from the ground," one said at the family door. "We can check it for free. Insurance will usually cover most of a new roof."

They promised upgrades, better shingles, and "almost no out-of-pocket" costs. Some neighbors shook their heads and closed the door. Others nodded and signed list forms, drawn by the idea of something new without writing a check.

Within a week, ladders leaned against several houses. Men in harnesses hauled bundles of shingles up and ripped off old ones. Nail guns snapped and crackled into the evening, louder than mowers and almost as steady. Tar paper and plastic wrap flapped in the wind.

Under all that noise, other rhythms slid back into place.

The minivan once again filled with backpacks and sports gear, heading out to fields and lessons. The single neighbor's TV glowed late into the night, storm coverage traded for shows and games. The retired son from the ornament house smoked on his porch, checked his siding for cracks, then drove off for his usual casino hours.

People talked briefly about how wild the storm had been. They compared hail sizes and told where they were when the lights went out. Then they went back to feeding the same habits storms could not reach.

From the porch, Lady Weatherwaddle considered what she had seen, and one night of shared darkness had fallen on every roof, every porch, every person. For a few hours, screens had gone blank, compressors rested, and the hum of machines gave way to rain and breathing.

As soon as power returned, the fill resumed. Light and sound rushed back to occupy every corner. The storm had dented metal and broken branches. It had not dented routines.

On this street, even the big weather became one more reason to purchase, repair, and upgrade. Roofers, generators, and insurance claims joined the existing pile of cars, gadgets, and boxes. The sky could shake the houses. It could not yet shake the way the people inside chose to live.

Chapter Seven

Chapter 7 – Late Nights and Blue Light

Night came late in summer, but the street did not wait for darkness to turn on its lights. One by one, windows glowed before the sky had entirely given up its blue. Inside, people leaned toward screens and turned their backs to the fading day.

Heat sat on the block even after dark, thick enough that the air-conditioners never really shut off. Blue light spilled from windows like extra lamps.

A few days earlier, when the first real heat wave settled in, the upstairs widow had dressed Lady for the whole summer. The duck wore a sleeveless white dress with fat red cherries painted along the bottom and a wide-brimmed hat tipped back from her beak. The widow moved carefully on the steps, pausing once with a hand to the rail, but she still fussed with the skirt until it fell in an even line. From the sidewalk, the outfit looked almost cheerful against the sagging, sun-bleached porch.

The single neighbor turned into the block later than usual, braking harder than he meant to. His car's front bumper already wore a fresh dent, paint scraped, and plastic warped inward. It was the kind of damage that came from a stop that came half a second too late. From her porch, the duck had seen that kind of thing more often as the years piled up on people.

He pulled into the drive and sat for a moment, hands still on the wheel. The cat, gray with a white chin, watched from the living room window and flicked its tail. When he finally got out, he moved slowly, shoulders rounded, eyes squinting against the last light.

He opened the trunk and dragged out grocery bags. Boxes and cans pressed against their sides. Frozen dinners, chipped beef trays, and pizza in bright cardboard slid onto his arms. A family-sized bag of Doritos rode on top, orange triangles peeking through the clear plastic, ready to stain fingers with artificial cheese and color.

He carried the bags inside, one hand fumbling with the keys, the other clamping everything against his chest. The cat wound around his ankles as he crossed the threshold. He almost tripped, then laughed once, without humor.

Later in the week, his trash would tell the same story as his groceries. Doritos bags crumpled into noisy balls. Ice cream cartons are slick with melted rings. Cans from soups and pastas that had never seen a fresh vegetable. A used vial or strip from diabetes medicine tucked among the junk, hinting at what all that processed sugar and salt had done to his blood.

Across the street, the single neighbor's living room lit up early and stayed that way. The TV bathed the walls in shifting blues and whites. The light moved with the scenes—a car chase, a game, a cooking show—flickering nonstop.

The cat stretched along the back of the couch, chin on paws, eyes tracking moths and bugs outside. Its litter box sat just off the kitchen, the smell faint but steady. When the neighbor cleaned it, he carried the plastic scoop and bag by hand. Granules and dust shook loose into the air and onto his skin. He wiped his fingers on a paper towel and reached for a snack.

"Just one episode," he told himself, settling onto the couch. "Then bed."

He tore open the Doritos bag and dug in, orange powder already smearing onto the remote. The TV was the only light on. The lamp nearby stayed off. The cat pressed against his leg like an extra cushion.

Outside, the rest of the block wound down in uneven stages. At the family house, the minivan arrived after practice, doors popping open like tired jaws. Kids trudged inside with bags slung low. Porch light blinked on, then off, then on again as someone remembered the trash.

At the young couple's place, the dog took a quick, final loop around the yard. It sniffed the same spots it had visited all day, each smell a little older now. Then it came back in, as the couple's faces turned toward a familiar movie.

In the lawn-ornament yard, the retired son eased his mother's wheelchair up the ramp. She had come back from her hospital or rehab stay thinner, her sweater hanging looser over her frame. He guided her to her spot near the window, tucked a blanket around her legs, and switched on the TV.

"There you go, Ma," he said. "Your show's on."

She nodded once, eyes on the screen, breathing shallow. He kissed the top of her head, then slipped back outside for a cigarette. The lighter's flare briefly lit his face as he leaned against the rail. Smoke rose between him and the street.

Then the night handed itself over to the screens.

In the single neighbor's living room, the TV no longer competed with any daylight. Its light ruled the room. He sat sunk into the couch, feet up on a crate that had once been meant for storage, a Doritos bag sagging in his lap. The cat pressed against his thigh, but his hand moved more often to the chips than to the fur.

"Just one more," he said as the episode ended and the next one queued up.

The screen's small timer ticked down in the corner: ten seconds, nine, eight. He lifted the remote, then let his arm fall. The next show loaded itself. The bowl he'd used earlier, once full of something microwaved from a box, sat abandoned on the crate—a faint neon sauce dried on the rim.

Time slipped by in small, forgettable slices. Watch a little, scroll a little. Check a message, laugh at a clip, forget what came before. The house glowed like a fish tank in a dark room.

Around ten, the traffic on the main street at the end of the block shifted. Daytime shoppers and commuters had thinned. The bars and late restaurants let out their own sounds. Farther down, near the corner, headlights swung as cars turned into and out of the lots.

Two Harleys roared up the main road, engines cracking the warm night air. Their noise bounced between the buildings, drifted into the side streets, then faded. A little later, a car with music turned up too high rolled past the cross street, bass thudding like distant thunder.

Some nights, the bar's small lot filled and spilled over. Cars lined the nearest side street and pushed onto this one. People used this block as overflow parking, trailing their laughter down the sidewalks. At two-thirty in the morning, voices sometimes lifted again—loud, unsteady, telling jokes and secrets in the dark as they walked back toward their parked cars.

The duck had heard those tones before, long before blue light became common. Alcohol gave words a particular slur and volume that carried. It made steps heavier and steering less exact, back then and now.

Tonight, the neighbor on the couch noticed none of it. The TV was louder. His eyes blinked more slowly. His fingers kept dipping into the chip bag until only crumbs remained. He licked them off, orange dust clinging to his tongue and nails, then reached for his phone.

At the family house, lights narrowed to one or two. A parent folded uniforms near a lamp while a phone charged nearby. At the young couple's place, one partner nodded off with a phone on their chest; the other kept scrolling through work email, mouth tight.

In the retired neighbor's house, the TV volume crept higher as his mother dozed in her chair. The son checked the time and counted the hours before the casino opened again tomorrow.

On some nights, the block's glow even split along channels. From one window, the sharp graphics and raised voices of a news panel show flashed red and blue bars; from another, a different network rolled endless breaking banners in softer colors. Lady could not hear the words clearly, only the tone—always urgent, always certain—and the way people's shoulders tightened the longer they sat in front of those screens.

In the single neighbor's living room, nothing dimmed.

The clock on the wall, barely visible in the flicker, inched toward one in the morning. The neighbor finally glanced up, rubbed his eyes, and yawned.

"I should go to bed," he said.

He stood and stretched, joints popping, then shuffled toward the bathroom. The TV stayed on. Its blue spill reached the hallway. In the bedroom, he picked up a smaller remote and pressed a button without thinking. Another screen lit the room.

He lay down with that light still pulsing against the far wall. The cat hopped up and curled near his feet. The ceiling flickered with reflected images, scenes of people in other houses, other cities, other made-up lives.

Sleep came in fits. He drifted, then snapped back when a scene changed or a commercial blared too loudly. The remote slipped from his hand, but his fingers still twitched, reaching for it even in a half-dream.

Outside, the duck watched the window rectangle stay bright while other windows faded. She did not know the name of the parasite that might hitch a ride on dust from cat litter. She did not see the ingredient list on the Doritos bag. She did know that this house rarely gave itself true dark or fresh air, and that its occupant moved like someone always a little off-balance.

At the end of the street, a pair of voices rose, laughing too loudly for the hour. Two figures staggered along the sidewalk, words slurring as they re-told a story from the bar. A car door slammed. An engine revved, louder than needed, and then the sound peeled away.

Add it all together, and the block did not sleep as much as it should.

Some people traded rest for light on a screen. Some traded it for alcohol and noise. Some traded it for late casino runs or extra rounds of mowing at dawn. Each routine looked small on its own, one evening at a time. Together, they carved hours out of the night and scattered them like chips bags and cigarette butts.

By dawn, the single neighbor finally fell into a deeper sleep, just as the sky lightened. The TV still flickered, now showing low-energy programs and long, boring ads. The cat left the bed and returned to the window, watching the street brighten.

The man on the couch in the retired neighbor's house stirred when the newscaster announced the time. The young couple hit snooze. The minivan family's alarm went off on a phone left plugged in on the kitchen counter. Coffee makers clicked and hissed.

Lady Weatherwaddle stood where she always did, bonnet slightly askew, eyes wide enough to take in the whole block. She had seen years of nights like this, different devices, same habits. People here wanted more energy, more focus, better health. They bought gear, pills, and trips trying to find it.

Then they stayed up too late under blue light, breathed stale air full of smoke and scents, and went into the next day already spent. From her porch, their tired routines looked like another kind of trash—harder to bag, harder to drag to the curb, but just as costly over time.

The street woke up again. Engines turned over. Doors opened and closed. The bright rectangles on the single neighbor's walls faded a little in the sun, but they did not go out.

Chapter Eight

Chapter 8 – Souvenirs and Short Breath

The day began in bodies that had not really rested. The duck watched them stumble into it, the same way she had watched them stumble into the night before.

Heat clung to the block like a damp hand that wouldn't let go. The afternoon sat heavily over the lawns and roofs, over the cracked sidewalk and the cars parked too close to the curb. Air shimmered above the blacktop, but most of the street had retreated inside, blinds half-tilted, blue light and air-conditioning humming behind glass.

On the porch with the lawn ornaments, the door opened slowly.

The retired son stepped out, one hand on the frame, the other braced on his hip. He squinted into the glare as if the day itself were too bright. His T-shirt clung to a softening belly that had grown year by year, the fabric dark where sweat had already seeped through. He moved more carefully than in earlier summers, joints stiff from disuse and old injury.

He paused on the top step to look over his kingdom: the trimmed grass, lined like a crew cut; the plastic edging pressed tight; the little collection of ornaments planted along the walkway. A gnome with a cracked hat leaned toward a frog that had lost one painted eye. A chipmunk held a faded "Welcome" sign that had never quite matched anything. Two spinning flowers made out of metal didn't spin much anymore.

Behind him, the screen door creaked, then eased shut. From somewhere inside, a television murmured at low volume.

Years back, he had gone off to work in the mornings like the other men, lunch in a brown paper bag, keys jingling, boots tied tight. The story on the street was that there had been an accident, or a bad diagnosis, or some mix of both. He had come home one day and just never gone back. Papers were filled out. Calls were made. Now the first of the month was its own kind of holiday.

He glanced toward the mailbox even though it was not the first. Habit made his eyes drift there.

On those days, envelopes came that mattered: his check, stamped with the language of disability; his mother's check; the small pension from the factory where she had worked decades ago, standing long hours on concrete floors while machines clattered and steam rose. The money arrived in thin paper, months stacked in memory like the piles of old mail on the kitchen table.

From the curb, her house did not look poor. It looked full.

Sometime between Memorial Day sales and the first fireworks stands popping up on the main road, the widow had made one more slow trip down the steps. She traded the cherry dress for a bolder red-white-and-blue outfit, stripes marching down the duck's skirt, and a tiny painted flag fixed to one wing. The colors no longer quite matched—fresh paint laid over old—but she straightened the little flag until it pointed neatly toward the street. On a block already buzzing with coupons and cookouts, Lady's Fourth of July dress joined the show without saying a word.d

He shifted his weight and shuffled down into the yard. The grass felt marvelously cool against his bare ankles. As he moved, a faint rhythm leaked from the car parked in the narrow driveway. A tune with bright accordion and quick drums floated out. It was the kind of music his parents used to play at weddings, church picnics, and the old social hall.
People used to clap in time and call it polka even when they couldn't name the language.

He let it play with the door cracked just enough. Maybe the neighbors heard it; perhaps they didn't. No one came over to ask.

The ornaments got his attention first. He brushed at one with a rag, smearing dust into a dull shine. His father had bought the first piece, back when the lawn still held a proper garden, tomatoes in a neat row, peppers staked straight, and herbs near the porch where his mother could reach them.

Now the garden beds were empty, turned to plain grass. The soil still remembered, even if most of the street did not.

From the front window, his mother watched.

The lace curtain bowed slightly where she leaned into it. Her shoulders were smaller than they used to be, swallowed by the print of her house dress.

Once, she had moved through the yard with a quicker step than his, bending and straightening without a sound, carrying baskets of beans and cucumbers back into a kitchen that smelled like broth, garlic, and fresh bread.

She had worked all day in the factory back then, then came home and worked some more,e stirring pots, rolling dough, stretching meals with cabbage and potatoes, and whatever had grown out back.

Now the yard was his, and the cooking came in foam containers.

He turned away from the ornaments and walked back toward the porch. The bulk of his belly shifted under his shirt. At the top step, he paused, breathing just a little more complicated than the walk deserved; the years since the injury had given him long hours and not much to do with them. The casino had solved that, in its way. So had the Dairy Mart up on the main road.

He glanced up the street where the sidewalk ran toward the busier corner. If the lottery were big enough, the store would already be busy with people willing to stand in the air-conditioned line and imagine new lives while the machine spat out numbered slips.

On jackpot days, he made that walk more than once. On Sundays, when the casino mailer arrived with its promises of a free buffet, bonus spins, and a chance at a drawing, he drove instead.

Losers went in the kitchen trash. Winners had never found a drawer to live in.

Behind him, a sound like a slight cough tapped the inside air. He pretended he hadn't heard it until he reached for the doorknob.

Inside, the house breathed a different heat.

Cool air moved from a window unit, just enough to keep the temperature down, not enough to move the curtain. The room smelled of scented cleaner, something floral that didn't exist outside, layered over old smoke that had soaked so deeply into carpet and upholstery that it would never really leave. Dust floated in a visible stripe where light snuck through the blinds.

The living room had shrunk over the years, not in size but in space.

Shelves clung to the walls, every one of them full. Porcelain figures posed under gray film: angels with gold-trimmed wings, shepherd boys, small girls holding baskets of painted fruit. Casino mugs from different years stood linedupw on the TV stand, each stamped with a logo and a year, promising luck that had never reached this address. A ceramic plate with a picture of the old country leaned behind them, its painted river too blue to be real.

Against one wall, a newer stack had grown. Boxes from the shopping channel stood half-opened, plastic wrap crumpled but not thrown away. A massager that made her dizzy. A cushion that was supposed to distribute weight and ease pressure points, now flattened where his body had pressed it instead. Comfort shoes are still in their packaging. A blanket that vibrated when plugged in, used twice, then folded for a "good day" that had never quite arrived.

His mother sat in her worn chair by the window, hands resting on a light blanket spread over her knees. Her ankles swelled against the elastic of her socks. The line from the oxygen concentrator curled like a pale snake from the machine at her side, across the carpet, up into her nose. When she drew breath, her chest rose shallow and small.

On the coffee table, pill bottles made a little city of orange and white.

He bent down to kiss her cheek. The scent of medicinal cream mixed with the powder she still dabbed on her neck out of long habit.

"Howare you doing, Ma?"

"I'm fine," she said, the way she always did, even when it wasn't true. "It's hot."

"The air's on." He reached up and turned the fan on the nearest lamp to its highest setting. It spun, blowing the warm air around more than cooling it.

In the kitchen, take-out containers crowded one corner of the counter. White boxes, folded over, holding last night's orange chicken and fried rice. A styrofoam clamshell with half a burger from the bar that also took his money on pull-tabs and keno. Plastic sauce packets gathered in a cup, lids sticky with sugar. When he opened the fridge, it offered cold soda, leftover pizza, and a tray of mashed potatoes from the grocery store's hot bar.

His mother had always said good food came from your own soil and your own stove. Now, despite the hospital visits and the warnings printed on the handouts they sent home, he went through the door with bags that smelled of salt, sugar, and grease.

Her body had grown heavier even as her arms thinned. He had grown soft from casino buffets, cheap hot dogs, and the endless plate of "free" food that came with points he'd bought dollar by dollar at the slots.

He filled a glass with ice water and carried it back, setting it within reach. Then he reached for the remote, flipping through channels until he landed on her game show. The familiar ring of the opening theme seemed to ease her shoulders.

"I might run out for a bit," he said casually, eyes still on the screen. "Use that coupon they sent. Just for a couple of hours."

Her mouth pulled down in a line he knew as well as his own reflection.

"You go," she said finally. "Just don't stay all night."

"It's double points until six. Be stupid not to go." He laughed lightly, as if making fun of himself could soften the truth of it. "I won't be long."

He checked the time. Almost three. If he left now, he could be back before the sun dropped behind the bank building on the main street. He placed the remote in her hand and set the phone on the arm of the chair. He straightened the blanket over her knees, tugged the line of her oxygen so it wasn't caught under the table leg.

"If you need anything, just call," he said.

She looked at him, eyes watering a little from the dry air. "I always need you," she said, half joking, half not.

He didn't answer. He stepped back out into the afternoon, shutting the door against the smell of old smoke and perfume, against the weight of the room.

On the porch, the heat hit like a soft wall. He pulled a cigarette from his pocket, tapped it against the box, and lit it with a practiced flick. Smoke rose to join the larger haze above the street.

Halfway down the walk, a delivery truck eased to the curb. Its brakes sighed as if tired.

"Got a package for you," the driver called, stepping down with a bulky cardboard box hugged to his chest.

"Yeah, I'll get it." The son stubbed out the cigarette, more from embarrassment than concern for his lungs, and met the man at the foot of the steps.

The box was heavier than it looked. The label carried the name of a channel his mother watched on quiet nights, the one with cheerful hosts and easy payments spread over months. The picture on the side showed a smiling woman reclining on a new device meant to make sitting easier, help her sleep more deeply, or dull pain.

"Another one," the driver said, not unkindly.

He grunted something like agreement and carried it inside. His mother watched him maneuver it through the door, eyes sharp despite the dull light.

"What is it?" she asked.

"Something for you," he said. "That cushion, they said, was good for your back. You remember?"

"Oh," she said. "I don't need it."

"You will like it. They said it helps." He set it down near the other boxes, promising himself he'd open it later. "We're just trying to make you comfortable."

The house seemed to sag under the weight of all the things meant to make life softer, even as her body made each breath harder.

He rechecked the time. Casino bonus hours weren't going to wait.

"I'm gonna go now," he said, back at the door. "You got your water, your pills, your show."

She lifted the glass a little to show him. He nodded, convinced more by his own momentum than by her gesture.

"Don't forget to lock the door," he added. "I'll bring you something back."

"Don't bring me junk," she replied. "Bring me something green."

"Salad," he said quickly. "I'll grab you a salad."

He closed the door on her laugh, on the soft wheeze of the machine at her side.

From her corner of the porch, the duck watched him walk toward the car. His steps were not relatively steady, guided by habit more than thought. He slid behind the wheel, the polka-beat drum kicking back in when he turned the key. The car eased out into the street, joining the slow stream of vehicles heading toward the strip of gas stations, bars, and glowing signs.

The day shifted around his absence.

Down the block, the minivan door slid open with its familiar stutter. A teenager stepped out first, hair dyed in streaks of purple and green that caught the light like oil on water. Another kid followed, dressed head-to-toe in black despite the heat—black shirt, black jeans, bracelets stacked up pale wrists. Their mother called something from the driver's seat about bringing in the groceries, about not leaving their stuff in the van.

They barely answered, earbuds in, faces turned toward the screens waiting inside. The older daughter—home from college for the summer—emerged from the front seat, phone in her hand, thumb moving. She wore a dress that hovered between casual and something else, and shoes that suggested she might not be home by dark.

An engine with more growl than the others rolled up to the curb. A blue Charger idled with the bass low, a figure behind the wheel leaning back like he had all the time in the world. The daughter checked the house windows once, then walked to the car. Her mother waved from the van, distracted by a ringing work phone and the mental list of dinner, laundry, and the next day's schedule.

The Charger pulled away, taillights briefly bright in the afternoon glare. They would not return that night.

From behind fences, a dog barked—a sharp, questioning sound. The young couple's dog next door answered, a quick yip near the back porch. Somewhere farther down, another dog chimed in, then another, their voices passing over the yards like a chain. To anyone listening closely, it might have sounded like a conversation; to most of the humans, it was just another piece of the background.

A train horn blew in the distance, long and low. Cars hissed over the main road a block away, their tires singing over worn asphalt. A jet traced its invisible line high above, the faint roar reaching the ground a beat late. Inside the houses, air-conditioners thrummed, televisions muttered, dishwashers gurgled.

People had learned to live above the noise. Only the sudden scream of an ambulance or the blast of a fire truck could still cut through.

Across from the duck, the single neighbor wrestled his trash can over the curb. The lid kept flopping back. A pizza box slid out, followed by a glossy bag from a drive-through and a bulk-size container of snack wrappers. One smaller bag hung lighter than the rest, a cluster of empty orange prescription bottles rattling against one another.

He pushed the whole can into place and went back inside without a glance at who might be watching.

Time thickened as the sun leaned slowly west. The block held its breath without noticing.

Inside the ornament house, breath was work.

His mother shifted in her chair, trying to find a place where her back didn't ache, and her hip didn't throb. The cushion beneath her thighs had flattened over months. The air felt too warm despite the machine. A cough rose without warning, clawing up from the depths of her chest.

She pressed a hand to her sternum and coughed, once, twice, again, each one dragging more air out than it brought in. The noise echoed in the room but went no further.

She groped for the glass of water, fingers clumsy on the slick condensation. It tipped, ice clinking against the side, but she caught it before it spilled. She took a small sip that did not help, then another, then rested her head back against the chair.

"Breathe," she told herself. "Just breathe."

The oxygen machine hummed on, indifferent. Next door, the young couple laughed at something on their screen. A lawn mower somewhere in the distance started up, its buzz hazy and far away.

After a long moment, her lungs loosened. The cough faded to a faint rasp. She wiped her eyes with the edge of the blanket and tried to pretend the episode had not scared her.

By the time her son's car rolled back into the driveway, the street had changed light. Shadows stretched longer from the maples. The heat had eased from punishing to merely heavy.

He got out slower than he had left. The smell of stale smoke and casino air clung to his shirt. A plastic bag hung from one hand; a crumpled mailer stuck out of his pocket. A faint ring of salt rimmed his hairline where sweat had dried.

He took the porch steps one at a time, pausing to catch his breath halfway up. At the door, he flicked ash from his fingers, though there was no cigarette there.

In the kitchen, he dropped the bag on the table. It landed with the soft thump of fried food disguised as dinner: chicken tenders, fries, a side of coleslaw, and a small plastic bowl of something green.

"Got you a salad," he called out.

"It's late," she replied, voice thin.

"Traffic," he lied, even though there wasrarelyr traffic at that hour for someone who knew which streets to take.

He emptied the trash while the microwave hummed. The bag filled quickly: glossy coupons, old mailers from the casino promising next month's deals, a broken figurine whose wing had snapped clean off, stale cookies from a tray he'd brought home free from the buffet.

He pulled up a handful of lottery tickets, smoothed one out as if a different angle might change the numbers, then crumpled it and tossed it in.

Near the top lay a small device still wrapped in clear plastic, the label claiming to ease back pain with gentle heat. He turned it over in his hand, frowned at the cord, and added it to the trash with a shrug.

"They said that one might help," his mother said from the other room. He hadn't realized she could see him from her chair.

"It's junk," he said quickly. "Didn't work."

"You never plugged it in," she pointed out.

He didn't answer. He tied the trash bag in a knot and carried it outside, shoulders hunched.

From the porch, Lady watched the white bag join the others at the curb, another offering to the truck that would come tomorrow and carry away the evidence of their days: the lost money, the wasted food, the tools of comfort no one used.

Later, after they had eaten what they could of the fried dinner and shoved the rest into the fridge, he brought out the photo album.

"Remember this?" he asked, sliding it onto her lap.

Plastic pages kept old summers trapped beneath them. There she stood in the yard with a trowel in hand, knees deep in tomato plants, hair tied back with a rag. There he was as a boy, face streaked with dirt, holding up a crooked carrot like a trophy. His father squinted against the sun, the lines around his eyes carved deep from smiling more than frowning.

"You worked too hard," he said.

She smiled at the memory. "We didn't have a choice."

He flipped pages. A black-and-white photo from the factory picnics. A shot of her in a hairnet, laughing, flour on her cheek in the kitchen. A vacation picture in front of a lake four hours away, a cooler just out of frame filled with sandwiches and homemade pickles. Trips bought with overtime, not luck.

He cleared his throat.

"I was thinking," he said, "maybe I'll get one of those little windmill things for the yard. The solar kind. They spin at night."

"You could plant something instead," she said, eyes still on the lake. "Something that grows."

"It's easier just to stick it in," he replied, not unkindly. "No weeding."

She closed the album after a few more pages, her hands tired. "I'm done," she said. "I'm tired."

He took it away and set it carefully on top of a stack of other albums, each one a weight of years.

As evening folded itself over the block, the last of the sun slid behind the roofs on the opposite side of the street. Lights came on in sequence, one house after another.

At the far end of the block, on the same side as the duck, the small house with the bright front door opened. Two women in their late twenties stepped out, laughing. One carried a laptop bag; the other jingled keys. Their clothes flashed color against the gray of the sidewalk—a yellow skirt, a teal shirt, an orange scarf flung over a shoulder, even in the heat.

An electric car hummed awake in the driveway, so quiet that the crunch of gravel under its tires sounded louder than the motor. Bumper stickers glowed on the back: Save the Earth, Love Is Love, Support Your Library.

They checked their phones, leaned toward each other to share a joke, then slid into the car. No one on the block had ever seen a boyfriend on their porch. The two women came and went together, schedules tight but aligned, like planets orbiting the same star.

Next door to them, the bigger house with the polished brick stood with its blinds half-open. A black sedan with tinted windows sat in the driveway, dustless. In front of it, a sports car rested low and sharp, paint shining as if it had just left the showroom.

The man who lived there stepped out in a suit that fit like it had been made only for him. His shoes gleamed against the concrete, a shine that spoke of care and money. He pulled a suitcase behind him, phone tucked under his chin as he talked about flights and time zones.

Later, another car would appear, bringing home the one who wore the jet pilot's uniform, wings stitched over the breast pocket, a bag slung over one shoulder, eyes tired from time spent above the clouds. Some weeks, they left in the morning; some weeks, they left at night.

Their lights blinked on and off at odd hours, and their bags were always either half-packed or half-unpacked—no kids, no regular schedule, just the rhythm of departures and arrivals.

The duck had watched them long enough to know that even when they were all home at the same time, the distance between their front doors never quite closed.

Neighbors passed each other with nods, not names. A raised hand from a driveway, a quick smile at a mailbox, then eyes back on screens, on steering wheels, on the path from car to couch. They lived close enough to hear one another's arguments and celebrations through thin walls, yet could have gone months without honest conversations.

Back inside the ornament house, the son turned up the volume on his mother's show so she could hear over the whir of the air unit. He adjusted her blanket again, though she hadn't asked.

"You need anything else?" he asked.

"I need what nobody can bring me," she said, then softened it with a small smile. "Go have your smoke."

He stepped onto the porch with his pack and lighter, letting the door close behind him. The lawn lay before him in its trimmed stillness, the ornaments standing in their silent parade. In the last light, their colors looked even more faded, as if the sun had been slowly drinking them for years.

He lit up and drew in, the smoke curling into the evening air. Across the street, television light flickered behind curtains. The minivan house glowed in both the living room and the kitchen, the trampoline now dark and still. The young couple's home showed a single square of light where they watched something side by side, but not speaking. The single neighbor's blue light filled his front window, one man and his device in an island of brightness.

From farther down, a car from the bar end of the main street rolled past, music up louder than it needed to be, bass thumping the quiet. Laughter drifted from its windows and vanished as it turned the corner.

Lady stood in her spot at the top of the steps, painted eyes fixed forward. She could not move, but she had seen enough summers to know the patterns.

Inside the ornament house, a woman who once fed herself from her own yard now depended on foam containers and plastic utensils. Her breath came in measured, labored sips. Her son, who had never quite stepped fully into his own life, fed the machines downtown with the money that kept them both afloat. His cigarettes burned down to ash as he admired a lawn that would outlast them.

On this block, people surrounded themselves with things that promised ease: cushions, take-out, tickets, screens, polished cars. They spent their hours chasing small bursts of excitement and comfort while time quietly thinned out underneath their days.

The duck watched the smoke rise, the lights blink, the cars pass, and held her place as the heat finally began to drain from the night.

Chapter Nine

Chapter 9 – Back to School and Busy Season

The air changed before the leaves did. Mornings came with a thin bite that slipped under door seals and into sleeves, making breath show faintly when people stepped outside too early. The light shifted too, lowering itself along the fronts of the houses so that porch rails and mailboxes threw longer shadows even before school started again.

Lady Weatherwaddle wore a new outfit to match it.

The upstairs widow had brought the clothes down in two slow trips: first the skirt over one arm, then the shawl and hat. She eased each step, one hand locked on the rail, the other hugging the bundle to her chest. The bright cherry dress of high summer went back into its bin. In its place, the duck now wore a soft tan skirt brushed with painted orange leaves and a darker shawl wrapped around her wings. A small felt hat, brown with a single acorn dabbed on the side, tilted over one eye.

"There," the widow had said when she finally tied the last knot. "Fall's coming, whether anyone's ready or not."

From the porch, it already looked like the season had grabbed the calendar and shaken it.

At the family house, the front steps turned into a pile of school and sports. Backpacks leaned in a crooked row against the railing, straps tangled and half-dragging. One bag bulged with notebooks and bright folders. Another sagged with gym clothes and a pair of shoes too clean to stay that way. A stack of forms, clipped together and half-filled, perched on the small table by the door, pen lying sideways on top like a tired flag.

"I printed the list," one parent called from inside. "Where are the headphones they wanted? And the calculator?"

"In the cart from last night," the other replied. "I told you—I put it on the card."

"Which card?" floated back, already sharp around the edges.

One of the kids stepped out, hoodie zipped despite the lingering warmth, backpack hanging low. The straps cut into their shoulders, and they shifted under the weight, trying to find a less painful spot that didn't exist. Another followed, heavier than last fall, breathing a little louder from the short climb to the porch. A pale blue inhaler stuck out of the side pocket of that backpack, plastic cool against the fabric.

"Did you remember my Chromebook?" they asked.

"It's in the bag," the parent said. "Just don't drop it. Do you know how much that thing costs?"

"I thought school gave them to us," the kid answered.

"Nothing's free," came the reply. "They just don't send the bill with the logo on it."

Across the street, the young couple's house woke to light instead of the sky. Lamps blinked on in the hallway before sunrise, their dog's nails skittering against the floor as it paced between the front door and the kitchen. One partner scrolled through emails at the table, spooning cereal without looking at the bowl.

The other juggled a laptop bag and a blazer, muttering about "fourth-quarter targets" and "busy season."

"We need to get on the day-care waitlist now if we ever want to sleep again," one said, almost joking.

"We barely see each other as it is," the other answered. "How would we even get there on time?"

The dog watched them both, head tilting at the rising tones, then returned to the window and fogged a fresh patch of glass.

Down the block, the single neighbor's curtains stayed half-drawn even as the sky brightened. Blue light from the television did more to mark the hour than the sun did. A new orange pill bottle now sat on the coffee table beside the remote, its crinkled pharmacy label turned toward the couch. Nearby, a folded piece of mail from a clinic poked out of a pile: the words "follow-up recommended" were just visible through the envelope window.

Outside, the street's moving parts clicked into place.

Garbage trucks rumbled past on their schedule, lifting cans that now held a new mix: empty sunscreen tubes, crumpled vacation brochures, and the plastic husks of back-to-school shopping—shoe boxes, blister packs from headphones, the spider-webbed plastic from toy hangers.

Roofing company stakes still bristled in a few lawns from the storm repairs, logos bright and proud in the cooler air. One yard carried an extra sign staked next to the contractor's: a rectangle of white with green and blue letters reading *Neighbors for a Kinder Future.*

Another house down the block had a smaller sign tucked near its porch steps: *We Welcome Everyone Here*. The duck could not read the fine print, but she knew the pattern. Signs sprouted and faded with seasons just like flowers, staking claims in soil while the same delivery trucks pulled up to every door.

Mid-morning brought the dog-walker wave.

First came the man from a few streets over who always wore the neon vest, three small dogs trotting at different speeds around his knees. They yanked at their leashes in turns, one darting toward a squirrel, one deciding to stop suddenly, one zigzagging purely for the joy of it. Plastic bags, already knotted and empty, bobbed from each handle, tapping his thigh with each step.

Not far behind him, two men walked side by side with three larger dogs between them. Their hair was cut close in the same way; their shirts fit the same way, bright against the dull sidewalk. One wore running tights under shorts. The other had a thin jacket tied at his waist, sleeves knotted neatly. Their steps matched without effort, leashes crossing and uncrossing as they traded grips, coffee cups, and a shared look when one dog tried to tangle them both.

At the corner, the lead dog made its usual veer toward the tree that marked the edge of the lawn-ornament yard. The lower trunk still showed its ring of damage—bark eaten away where salt, weed killers, and years of dog urine had burned it into a rough, dark band. What should have been clean gray wood now looked like a scar around the tree's middle. The dog lifted its leg, added another thin stream to the wound, and snorted with satisfaction.

"He loves that tree," one of the men said.

"Poor thing," the other replied, and reached over to flick a bit of stuck leaf off his partner's shoulder without breaking stride.

They moved on, three dogs weaving around their ankles as they had rehearsed it.

Behind them, a few more walkers came through. A woman in new sneakers and leggings marched with a tiny dog at the end of a bright retractable leash. Her cheeks flushed with effort as she checked the step counter on her wrist. At the slight rise of the sidewalk near the middle of the block, she puffed harder and slowed, then reached into her pocket and pulled out a wrapped candy bar.

She peeled it open in three practiced motions while the dog stopped to sniff the same bush it always did. From the porch, Lady watched the pattern: effort and habit taking turns, canceling each other out.

The poop bags all swung in time with their owners' arms—clean rolls in bright colors, and a few used ones already knotted and swinging low. Some got dropped into cans; others rode home in hands and pockets. Lady imagined a distant future, ae, a shovel scraping through layers of dirt, hitting all those tiny plastic bundles, sealed tight and still full. Whoever dug them up might decide this neighborhood had worshipped its animals, each offering wrapped carefully in oil-based cloth and buried along the curb.

Sunday rolled through the week like a speed bump more than a day of rest.

At ten in the morning, the church bell from a few blocks away still rang its thin line of sound over the roofs. Long ago, that note had pulled whole families past the porch: dresses ironed flat, small boys yanking at collars, Bibles tucked under arms.

Now, most weeks, only one or two households sent anyone on foot. A pair from the duplex at the corner might appear, walking with small steps and in careful clothes. Sometimes it was the sharp-suited man from the bigger house, keys in hand and face already set for the day. They usually left and returned in under an hour, as if faith itself had been squeezed into a tight appointment.

The rest of the block stayed in pajamas and T-shirts. Screens glowed behind their curtains while the bell still rang outside. Some shuffled to the kitchen for coffee and scrolled with one eye on the clock. From the porch, it looked like Sunday had turned into just another slow-starting workday.

Behind the trickle of church-goers, the four-person group with Bibles added its own small ritual to the block. Two men and two women walked in a neat line, shoes sensible, clothes clean but not showy. They had come from the same direction for years now, likely from a converted storefront that had grown a hand--painted cross above its door.

At certain houses, they stopped, climbed the steps, and waited with patient faces. At more and more doors, nothing moved behind the curtains. People sat on couches or at tables, ears tuned to football pre-game shows or streaming feeds instead of the knock.

"Next time," the minivan father said from his driveway when the group glanced his way. "We're just heading out."

They weren't. The van still sat half-unloaded from yesterday's tournament. But the bell and the group passed by all the same.

The rest of Sunday spun with a familiar, secular urgency. Laundry machines turned. Lists of chores got muttered and rewritten. Someone at the young couple's house shouted at a replayed call on a game. The retired son at the ornament house lined up his lottery tickets on the kitchen table and studied the numbers like they were a language he might someday learn. At the high-turnover rental, a new grill smoked on the porch while music leaked from a portable speaker, bass bumping along the siding.

Late one afternoon, the block received a jolt that did not come from a storm.

It started quietly. The single neighbor's TV had been on since morning; the sound was turned up a notch louder than usual. A game show gave way to a drama, then to the local news, then back to something else. Curtains stayed at their familiar half-mast. Now and then, the gray-and-white cat appeared in the window, then vanished again.

As the sun slid past the tops of the houses, a clatter inside that house cut through the TV noise. A dish hit the floor or a table tipped; Lady could not tell. The sound stopped as quickly as it had started. The show kept playing. Time stretched.

It was the cat that marked the change. It jumped into the window and paced, tail high and twitching, pawing at the glass in a way the duck had not seen before. It meowed, silent through the pane, again and again, then darted away and back as if trying to pull someone's attention inside.

Dusk moved in. Porch lights ticked on. The single neighbor's TV kept glowing, but no other shadow crossed that living-room window.

Much later, red and white lights spun silently down the block.

An ambulance eased to the curb in front of the TV house, brakes sighing. Two EMTs stepped out, bags in hand, faces already wearing the practiced blankness of people who had seen many evenings interrupted like this. They knocked once, then tried the handle. The door gave. The cat streaked out and under a bush as they went in.

For a long minute, nothing changed on the street. The minivan father stood frozen beside his garbage can, lid in his hands. The young couple paused on their porch, dog whining softly behind them. The retired son stubbed out a cigarette halfway and pocketed the butt without looking at it.

Inside, muffled voices rose and fell. Equipment beeped once, twice. One of the EMTs appeared in the doorway, calling to the driver. A stretcher came down the walk, wheels bumping on the uneven concrete.

The single neighbor lay on it, face pale, lips tinged with a color that did not belong on someone that age.

A thin line of dried orange dust marked one finger, caught in the crease near the nail. Electrodes dotted their chest. An oxygen mask fogged with each shallow breath. The new pill bottle rode in a clear plastic bag tucked by their feet. Someone said the word "stroke" into a radio, then again into a phone, voice flat but urgent.

The stretcher slid into the ambulance. Doors closed with a firm double thump. For a second, everything held still.

Then the siren snapped on, a brief wail before the driver cut it back to a lower, steady sound, leaving the block. Red light bounced off windows and metal for a few heartbeats and then swung away toward the main road.

The neighbors watched until the vehicle turned the corner. One by one, they went back to what they had been doing. Trash lids closed. Dog leashes snapped on. Televisions turned up to reclaim the sound.

Inside the single neighbor's house, the TV kept playing to an empty room. The cat crept back in through the still-open door and jumped onto the couch, curling in the warm dent where a body had been.

Night settled deeper.

Streetlights hummed. The church bell stayed quiet until next Sunday. The pill bottle sat on the table under the flicker of the ongoing show. No one on the block knew yet whether the neighbor would come back, or how different they might be if they did. Some would talk about it the next day at the mailboxes or over fences. Most would shake their heads, say something about "bad luck" or "health issues," and then push their own tired routines into the following week.

Lady stood where she always did, shawl catching small drafts of cool air. She had watched years of small habits stack up like the trash bags at the curb, light enough one by one, heavy when taken together. From her porch, this ambulance run did not look like a bolt from a clear sky. It looked like another bill coming due for a life paid out in little choices—food, screens, sleep, walks not taken past the end of the block.

September moved on around that absence the way the seasons always did. Backpacks still thumped down the steps. Dogs still pulled at leashes. Signs still leaned on lawns. The block's busy season rolled forward, one more time, over the same ground.

Chapter Ten

Chapter 10 – Bad Week in the Wind

The wind came back before the real cold did. It tumbled down the street in restless bursts, lifting leaves from gutters and lawns, sending them spinning across the cracked pavement. The first real layer of color lay on the grass—yellows and browns from the older trees that always dropped early, crunching softly under hurried feet.

Lady Weatherwaddle still wore her early-fall dress, but it looked a little too light now. The painted leaves on her skirt matched the ones piling at the edges of the sidewalk, yet the shawl over her wooden wings seemed thin for what was coming. Upstairs, the widow had coughed harder the last time she'd come down to straighten the hat. She had stopped twice on the way back up, one hand pressing the rail, the other against her chest.

Across the street, the lawn-obsessed neighbor added a new enemy to his list.

He had no tree of his own, just a tight rectangle of grass cut so short it looked shaved. The only trunk in sight belonged to the neighbor next door, a thick maple that had planted itself long before either of them arrived. Its branches arched over the property line in a lazy, natural shrug. Every gust sent a fresh wave of leaves down, plastering gold and brown against the perfect stripes.

The man came out three times that day with his rake.

He dragged the tines along the grass with sharp, angry strokes, gathering leaves into neat, accusing piles. The wind waited until he bent to scoop, then kicked half the pile back across the invisible line. He raked again. By afternoon, his yard looked briefly clear. Ten minutes later, the tree shook loose another shower. From the porch, it looked like the man was trying to argue with the weather.

He didn't glance once toward the maple's house. His glare stayed on the ground.

The delivery driver stepped around one of his leaf piles as if it were a sleeping animal.

They moved up and down the street with a practiced stride, box in each arm, scanner hooked at one hip. Their calves showed under shorts despite the chill, muscles knotted from hills and steps and truck ramps. Shoulders rounded only from weight, not from screens. They hopped from curb to porch with an easy balance that came from hours on concrete.

At one house, a resident commented from the doorway, "I wish I had time to go to the gym like you."

The driver gave a small smile, breath barely quickened. "This is my gym," they said, then jogged back to the truck for the following stack. All day, they walked and lifted while the street watched from behind glass or steering wheels, paying separate money to sit on machines that went nowhere.

At the high-earning couple's brick house, the sky and the driveway had their own quiet story.

The black sedan still came and went at odd hours, lights sweeping the front room and then vanishing for days. Its driver—pressed suit, shiny shoes, phone always at his ear—rolled his suitcase behind him and backed out of the drive with the effortless precision of someone who had practiced departures. The other car, the one the neighbors thought of as the pilot's, had not moved in almost a month.

One night, a third vehicle appeared.

A dark crossover eased into the driveway long after porch lights had clicked off. The streetlamp caught the clean paint and the flash of a license plate from another county. A woman in a well-cut coat stepped out, heels careful on the uneven concrete. She stood by the car for a moment, looking up at the brick front, then lifted a small overnight bag from the back.

The front door opened almost at once. The suited man stepped out, tie loosened, smile already in place. They exchanged a quick, familiar touch at the shoulder, then disappeared inside together. The car stayed until dawn, then backed out as quietly as it had arrived, taillights briefly washing the silent pilot car in red.

Lady had seen that pattern before in other houses over the years. Cars changed, faces changed, and overnight bags changed. The rhythm did not. Once, the pilot's car had been joined by flowers on the porch and luggage dragged in by two people; now, it sat alone while new wheels found room in the drive. The duck had no word for divorce or separation, but she knew the shape of people who stopped going in and out of the same door.

Down at the high-turnover rental, trouble was louder.

The house had cycled through so many couches, grills, and clusters of cars that it felt like a revolving door with siding. Lately, a group of adults had packed its small rooms, their voices carrying from the porch late into the night. Bottles clicked against railings. Music thudded just loud enough to irritate, not loud enough to draw a ticket.

On one wind-torn evening, the volume tipped.

A shout snapped across the block, harsher than the usual laughter. Another voice answered, higher and tighter. A crash followed—the sound of a glass or a plate shattering against something solid. The porch light flicked on and off in quick succession, then stayed on, spilling harsh yellow onto the rail.

Neighbors edged to their own windows, peering through blinds.

"Call them," someone muttered nearby.

A patrol car rolled up within minutes, lights off, engine low. Two officers stepped out, jackets zipped tight against the wind. They climbed the steps while the argument spilled through the thin door in a tangle of blame and old resentments. Words like "rent," "job," and "you always" floated out in broken pieces.

The door opened. The officers slid into the frame, voices dropping to that firm, practiced tone that tried to be both calm and absolute. The duck could not make out every word, but she knew the choreography. Hands spread. One person gestured wildly. Someone else stared at the floor. The officers left without cuffs this time, leaving behind a house that hummed with sullen silence instead of music.

The next morning, a red-bordered paper bloomed on the door.

A man in a red pickup pulled up, climbed out, and taped the notice to the window at eye level. He pressed the edges down hard, then snapped a picture with his phone before walking back to the truck.

The sign's printed words—about nonpayment and deadlines, about vacating by a specific date—flattened years of spinning tenants into a few lines of legal text.

The wind tugged at the corners. Someone inside opened the door, stared at the paper, and cursed under their breath. The notice flapped once, twice, then held.

At the ornament house, the wind found a different kind of thinness.

The retired son had been moving more slowly for days, shoulders drooping even when the weather was clear. His mother had come back from her last hospital stay with new pills and a slightly different chair, one that promised to tilt and lift when a button was pressed.

The nurse who delivered it had walked him through the instructions while he nodded, eyes darting between the machine and the clock in his head that counted down to casino promotions.

"Make sure she doesn't sit up too quickly," the nurse had said. "Watch for dizziness."

"Sure," he'd replied. "We got it."

They did not.

One gray morning, the blinds in that front window stayed shut longer than usual. The television flickered, but no silhouette shifted in the chair. The son did not appear on the porch for his usual first cigarette. The street went through its motions around that small silence: trucks, school buses, dog walkers, the leaf-raker starting his day-long battle again.

By mid-morning, a different van pulled to the curb. It was white, unmarked except for a small number stenciled near the door. Two people climbed out in dark jackets, carrying a slim stretcher folded in half. Their faces held no curiosity, only a weary respect that had repeated itself on too many blocks.

The son met them at the door, eyes rimmed red, hair flattened on one side as if he'd slept in a chair. He stepped back to let them in, then hovered in the doorway, hands opening and closing without anything to latch onto. From the porch across the street, Lady saw only brief shadows moving in his living room: a shape lifted, a sheet smoothed, a pause that felt like a held breath for the whole house.

They brought his mother out under a pale covering. She seemed smaller than she had sitting by that window, reduced to the outline of long years and short breaths. Her feet were hidden. Her hands were tucked. The son followed a few steps behind the stretcher, one hand reaching as if to touch the sheet, then pulling back at the last second.

"I'll lock up for you," one of the workers said gently.

He nodded without really seeing them.

The stretcher slid into the van with a soft mechanical whir. The doors closed without lights or sirens. This was not an emergency. It was paperwork now. The vehicle pulled away from the curb with a slow, respectful roll that did not match the tightness in the son's jaw.

He stood on the porch for a long time after the van turned the corner. Cigarettes went from pack to fingers to ash without him seeming to taste any of them. The television still murmured inside to an empty chair. The yard, which had always responded to his slightest command, waited without instructions.

The block shifted around that quiet.

Later that afternoon, the dog-walker with the wardrobe added color back into the street. A small brown dog trotted at the end of a leash wearing a bright red shirt stamped with a crooked logo: a made-up team name that meant nothing off a screen.

The next day, the dog came by in an Ohio State jersey, tiny sleeves flapping around its front legs. The day after that, there was a shirt that read something like "Best Boy on the Block" in glitter letters. The walker adjusted the hems carefully before each lap, paying more attention to cotton on fur than many neighbors gave to clothes on their own backs.

The leaf-raker worked all through those passes, raking the same stretch three times as the wind and the maple conspired against him. The delivery driver kept climbing the same steps, muscles carrying boxes to doors with red notices, sympathy cards, and credit statements tucked together in the same canvas bag. The high-rent house sat a little quieter with its warning paper. The ornament house sat much more peacefully without its second silhouette.

Night brought an early kind of dark.

The streetlights clicked on before most people had left work. Car headlights cut sharper cones through the cooling air. The young couple turned into their drive separately again, the dog howling a greeting for each arrival. The minivan slid into its spot, kids spilling out, complaining about homework and schedules. The single neighbor's window stayed dark;

their house now held only the sound of the TV, a visiting nurse's occasional footsteps, and the cat's soft paces.

On Sunday, the church bell's thin note still climbed into the wind at ten. Fewer feet answered it. The Bible group walked its route, pausing a little longer at some doors, glancing toward the houses that had seen vans come and go this week. They left a folded piece of paper on the TV screen, then moved on.

From her porch, Lady watched this bad week settle like another layer of leaves.

None of it felt like an accident. Old choices and new weather had rubbed together until something finally sparked. A smoker's mother, whose lungs had breathed the same stale air for decades, reached the end of her shallow pulls. Tenants who had stretched their money past its seams met a red line they could not cross. A couple that had once fit two neat schedules into one house now made room for a third set of keys.

The wind kept blowing. Leaves kept falling. People swept, taped, signed, and talked, then tried to fold everything back into normal. The duck, wrapped in her too-thin shawl, could feel winter pressing in behind this week, waiting to see what would hold and what would crack when the real cold arrived.

Chapter Eleven

Chapter 11 – New Porch, Old Weight

The cold settled in sideways, slipping under jackets and cuffs even when the thermometer still pretended it was only autumn. Wind worried at the edges of everything—loose shingles, half-rotted fences, sagging banners from forgotten festivals. It pushed leaves along the gutters in sudden rushes, then left them in damp clumps that stuck to concrete and shoes.

On the duck's porch, the boards now answered the weather with their own complaints.

They had been soft for years, but this season the give under a footstep had turned into a slow sink. The rail shook when the upstairs window leaned on it. Once, when she shifted her weight to cough, the post wobbled enough that she grabbed it with both hands and stayed still until her breath came back.

Not long after that, her children appeared.

They no longer lived in this house or on this block. They arrived in clean cars from better-kept suburbs, wearing jackets zipped tight and faces set in a mix of concern and impatience. Clipboards and printed estimates rode tucked under one arm. They tested each step with careful shoes, frowning when the wood answered too softly.

"This porch is a lawsuit waiting to happen," one of them said.

"Mom, we told you," the other added. "You can't keep putting it off. We're hiring someone."

The widow blinked, eyes moving from their lips to the boards and back again, as if trying to catch up to the conversation's speed. "It's held up this long," she murmured. "Your father built it."

"Forty years ago," one child answered. "Things rot. We'll get you something new. Safer."

The word "safer" came with the sound of phone calls and online searches, and a deposit made with a card that did not live in this house. Dates were set. A contractor's truck will come next week.

On the morning the work began, the widow insisted she could at least move the duck herself.

She came out wrapped in two sweaters, one buttoned crooked over the other. Her slippers showed a dark line where the porch had worn them year after year. She placed both hands on Lady's shoulders and rocked the statue gently until the base shifted free from the groove it had made in the wood. Then she rolled a rusty wheelbarrow close, metal squeaking in protest at every bump.

"Come on, girl," she said, as if the duck weighed nothing more than an armful of laundry. "We'll get out of their way."

It took three tries to tip Lady into the barrow. The duck landed with a solid thud, skirt and shawl askew. The wheelbarrow's single tire sagged sideways, air long gone. Still, the widow gripped the handles and heaved. The barrow lurched forward in short, uneven bursts around the side of the house.

Each shove left her more winded.

By the time she reached the backyard, she had to stop twice, pressing one hand to her chest, the other to the handle. The wheel bumped over a tree root and a forgotten toy half-buried in the ground. At the far edge of the yard, she eased the barrow against the wall of the detached garage and let the handles drop.

"There," she whispered. "You can watch from back here for a while."

She patted the duck's hat once and slowly made her way back inside, one hand trailing along the house siding for balance.

The backyard had its own world.

From this angle, the street was just a sound: the dull rush of cars on the main road, the occasional bark from the dog-heavy house, the far-off horn of a train rolling through a crossing she could not see. A plane's low drone crossed the sky from time to time, pulling a thin white line behind it that the wind smeared before it reached the horizon. No one on the block looked up at it anymore. They had heard that kind of noise so often that it now registered as silence.

The garage, though, spoke in other ways.

Its paint had peeled in sheets long ago, revealing gray boards beneath. The back wall bowed slightly inward where a gutter had failed, letting years of water trace the same lines down the siding and into the soil. From her wheelbarrow, Lady could see through a cracked pane into the dim interior.

Old things filled every inch.

A dining table leaned sideways against a dresser, one drawer missing. Two refrigerators, long unplugged, sat like white tombs under a blanket of dust and spider webs. Boxes of cotton fabric and old clothes towered in teetering stacks, lids bulging with the weight of saved seasons. A brass bed frame leaned against the far wall, speckled with rust, its curls still trying to look fancy in the dark.

There was barely enough space for a narrow path to thread between everything.

From inside that back wall came a faint, constant noise—too soft for human ears hurrying past, but evident to a painted bird with nothing else to do. A dry, uneven scritching, like someone slowly tearing thin paper behind the boards. Termites worked their long, secret lines through wet, softened wood. The gutter had dripped just enough for just long enough to feed them, and now they chewed their way forward in patient hunger.

The garage held onto everything the widow could not bear to let go of. The house let go of itself in the meantime.

Later that morning, the workers arrived with their promise of "maintenance-free."

An extended trailer backed into the drive out front, unseen by Lady but loud in its beeping and grating over the curb. Voices called measurements back and forth. Boards thudded onto sawhorses.

The new porch came in stiff, perfect planks wrapped in plastic, each piece identical to the last. When one of the workers tore open a wrapper, a sharp chemical smell bled into the air, slipping around the house and into the backyard on the same breeze that carried the scent of wet leaves.

"Composite," one man said proudly. "Never rots. No splinters. You'll never have to replace this again."

"Good for resale," another added.

Saws whined. Synthetic dust floated on the wind, catching in the low autumn light. It mingled with the natural sawdust from the old porch boards they ripped up and tossed into a growing pile. The new "wood" would outlast the widow, the kids, maybe even the whole house. It would not feed a single termite.

The wind grew stronger as the day leaned toward afternoon.

It rounded the corner of the house in gusts that threatened to tip the wheelbarrow. Leaves and bits of paper rode the currents, skittering along the fence until they caught in chain-link or hedges. From the main street came a sudden, unmistakable smell—grease and char and the specific sweetness of corn syrup in a bun. Burger King Whoppers sizzled somewhere down the road, their smoke funneling out of rooftop vents and sliding along the low sky until it reached this yard.

For a moment, the backyard smelled like a grill at a tailgate.

On the other side of the fence, a long line of dog barks rippled and overlapped, each voice layered on the last until it became one rough chorus. A train horn blew again in the distance. A plane dipped lower on its approach to the airport, engines humming louder. No one on the block stepped outside to notice any of it. They had laundry to change, emails to answer, steps to count, and games to watch.

At the high-turnover rental, the week's earlier drama moved into its next phase.

A battered F-150 rolled up, paint faded, and bed already scarred from years of hauling. Two men jumped out and headed straight for the front door, not bothering with the broken steps they had climbed so often before. The red eviction notice still flapped on the frame, corners curling inward. One man ripped it off and crushed it into his pocket without reading.

Inside, the house released its latest contents in armfuls.

Mattresses stained with shapes of old sleep. A TV with a cracked corner, screen still smudged with fingerprints. Black garbage bags stretched tight around clothes and who-knew-what else—a lamp, its shade bent, its cord dragging on the step. Chairs went into the truck bed back-first, legs sticking up like broken insect limbs. Some items were handled carefully, others thrown hard enough to bounce once before settling.

The truck is filled. The men climbed in, slammed doors, and pulled away with a squeal.

By late afternoon, a different car slid into the empty drive—a small sedan with a magnetic sign on the door and a folder-holding woman inside. She unlocked the front door and ushered a new pair through, smiling widely as she talked about "potential" and "up--and-coming area" to people who glanced at the scuffed floors and patched walls with more doubt than hope.

Across the street, the ornament house sat in a quieter kind of transition.

The retired son no longer pushed a wheelchair up the ramp. The front window's chair faced the television alone. Sympathy cards lined the sill in uneven rows, their glitter and cursive words catching stray light. The son appeared on the porch now by himself, cigarette already lit. Smoke curled around his head like an extra, thinning scarf.

He talked on the phone with short, impatient sentences.

"Yeah, I filed it," he said. "They said six to eight weeks on the check."

A pause.

"I'm taking care of it, okay? Just—just let me handle it."

That night, his car left for the highway at the same hour it always had. The casino's rhythm had not changed with the house's. The duck could not see the bright machines and windowless rooms, but she could feel the repeated pattern in the way his taillights turned the same corner, the same way, on the same days.

At the young couple's house, another kind of absence had grown.

For weeks, only one of their cars had moved in and out. The dog had worn a path between the front window and the couch, restless in a way the duck had not seen before. Packages with medical logos had begun to appear on the porch among the meal kits and online orders, boxes that rattled differently when the delivery driver set them down.

One afternoon, a rideshare car pulled up instead of the familiar sedan.

The missing partner stepped out slowly. Her clothes hung looser on her frame. A patterned scarf covered her head, but a hint of plasticky hairline showed where a wig sat just slightly crooked. She held a canvas tote with a clinic's name printed in soft blue letters, the corners of the bag stiff from newness. When she reached up to steady herself on the porch rail, the sleeve of her sweater slipped back enough to show the faint, angry line left by a hospital bracelet.

"You okay?" her partner asked, voice gentler than the duck had ever heard it.

"I'm fine," she lied. "Just tired. They said round two might hit harder."

They stood together on the porch for a minute, shoulders touching, both staring out at nothing in particular. The dog pressed its nose against the glass, whining, tail wagging with a joy that did not match its face.

Inside, the television would come on that night to some show about health, cooking, or crime. On the table, beside unopened cookbooks and fitness bands still in their boxes, the clinic tote would sit like another product in the mix—this one for a body pushed too far for too long.

Farther down, the electric car house glowed with its own kind of urgency.

Through the front window, cardboard, markers, and paints covered a wide table. Two women leaned over it, sleeves pushed up, laughing as they argued over letter spacing and colors. Wine glasses with a pale liquid sweated beside bowls of hummus and cut vegetables. A speaker played quiet music under their voice.

"'Protect Our Home Planet' is too long," one of them said. "It won't read in photos."

"What about 'This Is Our Only Home'?" the other suggested, brushing in the words with careful strokes. "Shorter. Still true."

Hand-drawn earths, hands, and hearts bloomed on the signs spread across the table. They moved in practiced tandem, trading brushes and markers, bumping shoulders, pausing to share a smile or a private joke. No meat sat on their plates. Their shoes were without leather. Their refrigerator, if opened, would reveal oat milk and greens, with tofu blocks stacked between the containers.

Later that week, they walked the block with finished posters rolled under their arms.

"Hey, neighbors," one called, knocking gently on the minivan door. "We're going to a march on Saturday: climate, health, all that. Want to come? We're making a carpool list."

"Sounds great," the tired parent said, hand still on the doorframe. "We've got a tournament that day. Maybe next time."

At the ornament house, the son opened the door a crack, cigarette already in hand.

"Can't," he muttered. "Gotta be somewhere."

At the TV house, the nurse answered and smiled politely. "She's not up to crowds," she said, nodding toward the recliner inside. "But we'll watch on the news."

The women thanked everyone anyway and moved on, their signs swinging at their sides, slogans and drawings ready for cameras far from this street.

The dog-walker parade continued beneath all of this, unchanged.

The small brown dog in shirts came by each day with a different message. One morning: an Ohio State jersey, double-zero on the back. The next: a bright green top that read "Rescue Dogs Rescue Us." Another: a red shirt with a made-up logo, some paw-print team that existed only on cotton. The walker brushed each outfit smooth before leaving the driveway, fingers lingering on seams and slogans.

The candy-bar woman moved more slowly now, a soft brace hugging one ankle under her pant leg. She still carried her step counter on her wrist. She still stopped at the same small hill to catch her breath. Her hand still found a crinkling wrapper in her pocket even as she checked the numbers on her device. The dog danced ahead, nose to the ground, as if the walk were enough for him, no matter how many minutes it lasted.

The delivery worker remained the same, if slightly more layered.

Now a thin jacket covered their arms, but the stride did not change. Boxes rose and fell against their chest in a steady rhythm. Calves pushed upthe steps with the same easy power as in summer. They dropped packages on new porches and old, in front of red notices and fresh flowerpots, at doors with "Welcome Everyone" signs and doors with no signs at all. Their day was eight hours of moving weight. Few people made it to the door fast enough to see the muscles doing the work.

One morning, a neighbor joked, "You must not need a gym membership."

The worker smiled. "Can't afford one," they said. "But I get my steps."

A thin frost glazed the roofs one night and left a warning on the steps.

At the duck house, one of the widow's children came by early to check on the new porch. They stepped out without looking down. Their foot hit the first tread and slid. Hands flew up; a shout tore out of their throat. The new composite rail caught their grip, arm yanking hard, shoulder complaining.

"Whoa," they gasped, heart racing. "Almost broke my neck."

They laughed shakily and pulled out their phone to text a sibling about salt and mats and maybe a non-slip strip. The near fall became another item on a list, not a reason to slow down.

Later that day, sirens screamed along the main road and cut across an intersection beyond the houses. Heads turned for a moment as the sound rose and faded, but when it did not swing onto this block, people returned to their rakes, screens, and chores. The emergency belonged to someone else this time.

In the backyard, Lady sat in her wheelbarrow, dress wrinkled from the awkward angle, hat slightly askew from a sharp gust.

From here, she could not watch every footstep or see every new sign. She could, however, see the garage sagging a little more at its back corner. She could hear the termites working, their steady, invisible destruction powered by a leak no one had fixed. She could see dust gathering on things that had once been precious enough to save, now too tangled to sort.

She imagined the widow's children years from now, when some final paperwork demanded that the house be emptied. They would stand at the garage door, overwhelmed, then call someone with a bigger truck. The path would vanish under fast decisions. Furniture, fabrics, fridges, bed frames, and any small statue unlucky enough to be near the wrong pile would tip into a dumpster without ceremony.

From her perch, the duck thought about how quickly people could throw away a lifetime of saved objects when forced to decide, and how slowly they were willing to throw away a single bad habit when there was still time to change it.

The block had added new porches, new signs, new slogans, and new scars this season. It had lost a mother and gained a diagnosis. It had traded old wood for plastic that would outlast its owners and patched small cracks while bigger ones spread out of sight. Through it all, most people kept moving at the same pace, eyes on the next bill, the next shift, the following notification.

If any of them had stood still long enough to see the pattern the way Lady did, watching the years stack up like boxes in a crowded garage, they might have shifted something in their own lives while there was still space.

Instead, the days filled, the storage filled, the schedules filled. The only empty places on the block were the ones where someone had finally left, and no one had moved in yet.

Chapter Twelve

Chapter 12 – Dumpster Snow

Snow came in layers that year, not all at once. It arrived as dust first, a light powder that settled on the patched roofs and composite porches, filling hairline cracks and softening the hard edges of trash cans. Then it thickened, storm by storm, into banks along the curbs and gray ridges where plows had pushed it into tired piles that never fully melted before the next wave.

Lady Weatherwaddle watched the change from the wheelbarrow in the backyard.

The widow had never come back to move her. After that last, careful trip around the side of the house, the old woman's footsteps had grown rarer and then stopped altogether. Extra shadows had appeared behind the upstairs curtains—children's faces, once in a while, and a stranger's.

One bitter morning, a plain white van had eased up to the house and taken her away under a sheet, as quietly as it had taken the ornament mother a few weeks before. The duck had heard the murmured words, the brief weeping on the porch, the door closing with a firmness that sounded like an ending.

Now the yard belonged to snow and silence.

Drifts leaned against the back of the garage, smoothing its bulging wall into a single crooked curve. The cracked window glazed over with frost, blurring the stacked shapes inside—furniture, fridges, boxes of fabric—into lumps and shadows. From beneath that wall, the faint scritching of termites still carried through the wood, slower in the cold but not stopped. They worked on while everything else shivered.

The wheelbarrow had collected its own coat. Snow packed into the basin around Lady's skirt, crusting hard where daytime thaws met night freezes. Her painted leaves and shawl peeked through in places, the acorn on her hat wearing its own cap of ice. Wind drove powder into her bonnet ribbon. She could not see the street now, only the fence line, the garage, and a rectangle of sky that changed color without changing much else.

The sound of the street still reached her.

Engines coughed awake each morning, grinding through the cold until they found their rhythm. Dogs barked in their usual uneven chorus, voices muted by closed windows but still stacking into a familiar pattern. Somewhere beyond the houses, trains moaned and clacked over winter tracks. Planes shifted to a deeper, more distant hum, their lights tiny smears in the low, dirty clouds. None of it made anyone pause. These noises had become the block's lullaby.

One morning, a heavier rumble shook the yard.

A roll-off dumpster slid into the driveway out front, its steel belly banging against the frozen pavement. Chains rattled. The truck's reverse beeper pierced the air in harsh, insistent bursts until the container finally came to rest with a hollow boom. Snow shook from the garage roof in a loose cascade.

The widow's children had come back with purpose.

Their voices floated around the side of the house, crisp in the cold.

"We have to get this done before closing," one said. "The realtor said they already have offers."

"Just toss it," the other answered. "If we start sorting, we'll be here until spring."

They opened the garage door for the first proper time in years. Hinges groaned. The door rolled up in jerks, letting a wave of stale air spill out—a thick mix of old cloth, dust, and refrigerator rubber that had outlived its plug. The wind pounced on it, tearing the smell apart and carrying it across the yard.

"God," one of them coughed. "How did she even walk in there?"

"She didn't," the other said. "She just kept stacking things closer."

They began with the easy decisions.

Broken chairs sailed into the dumpster first, landing with hollow bangs that echoed off the neighboring houses. A cracked dresser followed, drawers still full of tangled scarves and slips. The old refrigerators went next, doors strapped shut, shelves rattling inside. Boxes of cotton fabric and holiday linens flew in armfuls, patterns and colors flashing once against the gray sky before disappearing over the metal lip.

Each throw shook something loose.

At the back wall, freed from the counterweight of piled furniture, the termite-eaten boards bowed inward under snow and age. One section gave up with a muffled crack. A chunk of siding slipped, exposing darker, softer wood beneath and a slit of the world inside. Snow sifted through like flour, falling onto the rusted bed frame and a stack of magazines promising better homes than this one.

"We'll have to tell the inspector about that," one child muttered, staring at the sag.

"We'll say we didn't know," the other replied. "We honestly didn't."

They moved faster.

The path through the garage narrowed, then vanished. Boxes with half-legible labels—"XMAS," "BABY CLOTHES," "CRAFTS"—landed in the same indifferent he—a A lamp with no shade. A crock-pot still wrapped in a brittle plastic bag. A stack of clown--faced cookie tins that had never seen a cookie. None of it paused their arms for more than a heartbeat.

In the backyard, their eyes finally landed on the wheelbarrow.

"Remember this thing?" one said, tapping the barrow's handle with a boot. "She loved that stupid duck."

"It scared me when I was little," the other answered. "Why did she keep this and not throw away the junk mail?"

They both laughed once, breath hanging in the air like faint smoke.

"You want it?" the first asked.

"Nope," the second said. "You?"

"Hard pass."

Together, they heaved the wheelbarrow forward, snow cracking and sliding from its edges. The tire bumped and squealed over frozen ruts as they steered it around the house. In front, the dumpster's open mouth waited, rim dusted white, metal sides already scraped and dented from earlier throws.

"Watch your back," one said, gripping the handles.

On three, they tipped.

Lady went up, then over. For a moment, she hung against the sky, hat tilted back, shawl flaring as far as frozen paint allowed. Then gravity claimed her. She crashed down into the mix with a sound that cracked a chip from her base. Splintered wood, bent metal, and fabric swallowed her in a cold embrace. Above, the rectangle of sky shrank to a frame around snowflakes and distant chimneys.

"Another load done," one child said, wiping gloved hands on their coat.

"Almost there," the other answered. "I just want this all gone."

They walked back toward the garage without looking down again.

From inside the dumpster, sounds came from a different angle.

Cars still started. Dogs still barked. Somewhere, a snow blower whined to life in a high, insistent pitch. The leaf-raking neighbor, who had spent whole afternoons in fall battling someone else's maple, now marched up and down the sidewalks with a brand-new Toro. He wore a fresh coat, a newer hat, and gloves that still showed store creases. The machine spat lines of snow off the concrete in two clean directions, clearing not just his walk but the one on either side as well.

He had more time now. And, it seemed, a little more money.

The ornament mother had left something behind other than sympathy cards. The son's new car, parked proudly in his drive, shone even under salt spray. He still smoked on the porch alone, shoulders hunched against the cold, but his machine roared down the street with new confidence when he headed toward the highway and its rows of glowing signs.

One storm dropped a wet, heavy snow that clung to everything it touched.

A compact car out front tried to plow through a drift and failed, tires whining in place until the rubber burned. Its driver, coat flapping open, pushed against the hood while the engine complained. The wheels dug deeper. A neighbor trudged over with a shovel and some old cardboard. Another arrived with jumper cables after repeated starts drained the battery. Together, they grunted and cursed and laughed a little when the car finally lurched free, water and slush soaking their socks inside their boots.

"Thanks," the driver said, breath steaming. "I owe you one."

"Nah," came the answer. "Happens every year."

Nothing about the interaction changed how anyone would drive the next storm.

In between loads, a familiar F-150 eased next to the dumpster, its engine rumbling low.

The man who climbed out wore the same thick jacket Lady had seen at the high-turnover rental. He hoisted himself onto the snow-dusted rim with the grace of practice and peered down into the chaotic pile.

"Mind if I look?" he called toward the house.

"Take whatever you want," one of the widow's children shouted back without turning. "Less for us."

He started picking.

A small table with a single wobbly leg was moved aside for repair. A metal tin with a decent lid followed, its clown faces dented but still cheerful. A box of fabrics made a soft thud in the truck bed. He came and went like this over several days, each visit coinciding with a fresh layer tossed in by the family, taking what others had decided they could not keep.

On his third trip, his boot nudged something solid under a drift of clothes.

He dug with his gloved hands, pushing aside scarves and a cracked picture frame until his fingers met painted wood. Lady's hat emerged first, then her stiff shoulders, then the full weight of her base. He blinked, then laughed once.

"Well, look at you," he said. "You're a beast."

It took effort to wrestle her upright in the cramped space, then lift. Muscles in his arms and back bunched under his coat. He dragged her to the rim and tipped her slowly over, careful not to let her crash onto the truck.

"You'll clean up nice," he muttered, easing her into a corner of the bed. "Somebody'll want a porch duck. Folks always do."

He wedged her between a mattress and an old dresser to keep her from sliding, then climbed down and brushed his gloves off. Snow began to fall again, fine and steady, dotting her bonnet and the truck's already scarred sides.

While all this moved in and out at the widow's house, the rest of the block kept its own weather.

At the high-earning couple's former place, the "For Sale" flyer at the curb had already grown a red "SOLD" banner—a moving truck parked once, then again, carrying out sleek furniture and carefully wrapped art. The suited man loaded boxes alongside the well-dressed woman, who had started appearing at night months earlier. Their goodbye was quiet—no party, no gathering, just one last turn of the key and a locked door.

Soon after, a different vehicle pulled up: an older van, doors stuck a little, kids' faces pressed against windows.

An Asian family poured out of it in a flurry of coats and bags. Five children tumbled onto the frozen lawn, arguing over who got which room they had not yet seen. The parents looked up at the brick, then down at the cracked sidewalk with a mix of hope and calculation. Within a week, new bikes lay on their sides near the porch, and a plastic slide appeared in the yard. The delivery trucks found the address automatically. The school bus learned new names at the morning stop.

On a nearby porch, two neighbors talked while they watched the F-150 climb the dumpster again.

"Did you hear about that photographer on Hilliard?" one asked, breath puffing.

"The one who used to do school pictures?" the other replied.

“Yeah. They found him last week. No heat, no water. Just... froze in there. Business went under when everyone started using their phones. No one checked on him for days.”

“Awful,” the second said. “And over on Westwood, that kid—fentanyl or whatever. Twenty-two. His mom works with my cousin. She said he was just... gone when the ambulance got there.”

They shook their heads, then changed the subject to snow parking bans, new trash pickup rules, and whether school would be delayed again.

At the TV house, a fresh dent decorated the single neighbor’s front bumper.

He told anyone who asked that he had slid on black ice when the car ahead of him stopped short. His laugh carried a thin note of embarrassment. Underneath his words lay other truths: late-night TV, poor sleep, sugar, pills, and the subtle fog that came from years of cleaning a litter box in the same small space where he lived and ate. The cat, ageless in the window, watched birds and falling snow as if nothing had shifted at all.

The minivan family's kids kept eating as their schedules allowed.

Canned soup, boxed macaroni, frozen chicken nuggets, and microwaved breakfasts passed across the table in a blur between practices and homework. One child seemed to catch every cold; another had grown a soft ring around their middle that no amount of rushed gym class could touch. A third now takes a small pill every morning for reflux in a throat not yet old enough to vote. Their parents traded late-night conversations about "insurance," "co-pays," and "we'll do better after this season," even as new receipts piled up.

Dog walkers still traced their winter paths.

The two of us, known with three dogs, wore thicker coats and knit caps, their leashes looped around gloved hands. The lead dog still pulled toward the same tree, now burdened with a crooked halo of dead branches where bark had cracked and failed. Yellow spots dotted the snow around its base like a map of old stops. The tree seemed to lean away from the sidewalk as if trying to escape its duties.

The small brown dog in shirts now added booties to its wardrobe, click-clacking delicately over ice in tiny rubber soles. One day, its torso proclaimed "Snow Day Champ"; another day, "Adopt

Don't Shop," in puffy letters. The owner laughed when strangers smiled, tugging the coat straighter before each lap.

On one particularly sharp Sunday, the smells and sounds layered thicker.

The lesbian couple—the two women with the electric car and vegan snacks—left early with rolled banners and their best coats. Their signs read "Protect Our Only Home" and "Health Over Profit" in careful letters. The church bell rang its thin, determined note at ten as they drove off toward the march. The usual pair of church walkers stepped by in its wake, collars turned up, Bibles tucked under arms, shoes crunching on salted walks.

Later, the four-person Bible group came down the street again, breath showing in small puffs as they spoke. They paused at the pilot's old house, now bright with new toys and five sets of tiny boots lined up at the door. The father opened the door to their knock, children tumbling in the background.

"Welcome to the neighborhood," one of the visitors said, genuine warmth in their voice. "We're from the church down on Madison. If you ever need anything..."

The man smiled politely, nodding, eyes already darting toward a pot on the stove or a child behind him.

"Thank you," he said. "We're still unpacking. Maybe once we're settled."

They left a folded pamphlet and moved on, boots squeaking, glancing up once at the For Sale sign still planted across the street in front of the widow's now-empty house.

By afternoon, the lesbians returned from the march, faces pink from the cold, voices hoarse from chanting. They unloaded their signs back into the garage, hung wet scarves over chairs, and scrolled through photos on their phones of crowds and speeches and themselves, tiny and bundled among thousands. On television in another house, someone summarized the same event in ninety seconds between insurance ads and fast-food commercials.

As the short winter day drained of light, the man with the F-150 finished his last dive into the dumpster.

One more small table, one more box of old glass jars, one more bundle of fabric went into his truck. Lady rode in the corner, bonnet now crusted with a mix of snow and scratched paint. When he slammed the tailgate and climbed into the cab, the engine's vibration ran through her base in a new way. She could feel the old street only as a shift and a tilt now, not as a fixed stage beneath her.

The truck pulled away from the curb.

From her low angle in the bed, she caught slivers of familiar things on the way out: the top of the diseased tree, the edge of the new plastic porch, the shadow of the ornament house's front window, one last flash of the minivan's roof. Somewhere behind her, the dumpster still yawned, half full of what had once filled a life. The For Sale sign waited for a new name.

The street did not stop to watch her go.

Engines idled. Televisions glowed. The church bell fell silent for another week. Dogs barked at nothing and everything. Somewhere nearby, a cat used its box. Farther away, sirens wailed for someone else's crisis. The snow kept falling in small, steady flakes, covering footprints and tire tracks, softening sharp corners, hiding the difference between what had just arrived and what had just left.

As the truck turned onto the wider road, Lady understood that nothing she had seen here would stay exactly as it was, but almost everything would repeat. Houses would change hands. Cars would spin out and be towed, then replaced. Children would grow, move out, come back, move again. Some people would collapse under the weight of food, light, and debt. Others would march for change between long, screen-lit nights. Most would keep hurrying past the edge of their own lives, too busy to stand still and look.

She could not know yet what the next block would bring, only that wherever the truck stopped, there would be other houses, other porches, other dogs, other screens. Other people rushing, eating, collapsing, protesting, praying, gambling, scrolling. Another chance for someone to stand as still as she did and watch long enough to see the pattern.

The truck's taillights glowed red against the white as it carried her out of the neighborhood and into whatever story waited beyond the snow.

Chapter Thirteen

Chapter 13 – The Last Street

By the time the F-150 rumbled behind the strip mall, Lady had stopped expecting anything new.

The bed was piled high: broken chairs, a dead treadmill, three black bags from a college move-out. The man in the ball cap heaved up one more bag from the dumpster and heard a hard clunk against the metal floor. When he dragged it open, a blue suitcase tumbled out and thudded onto the truck.

He wiped grime off the lid with his sleeve. The latches still worked.

Inside, folded like someone still meant to go on vacation, were Lady's clothes.

The yellow slicker. The Fourth of July scarf. The Easter bonnet with the crushed silk flowers. A faded football jersey. A crooked pair of sunglasses. It was like opening a time capsule from a porch that no longer existed.

"Well, look at you," he said, half to the suitcase, half to the plastic bird watching from the corner of the truck bed. "Match set."

He took her home.

Two days later, after a rinse in the driveway and a rag over her beak, Lady stood in the front window of his second-hand shop, balanced on top of the blue suitcase like a cheap department-store model.

Window watchers

From here, the river changed.

Instead of one short street, there was a steady flow along the cracked sidewalk: strollers, shopping bags, backpacks, borrowed grocery carts.

Kids licked ice cream and dropped the last inch on the pavement. Dogs yanked owners toward smells, toenails scratching over the concrete, tiny jackets flapping. A man pushed a woman in a wheelchair, an oxygen tank in the basket, and a store bag hooked to the handle.

Most people didn't look up. Their faces glowed blue from screens, or pinched around a phone call, or slackened with the tiredness that comes from working and buying and working again.

Lady watched them the way she had watched the old block: how they moved, what they carried, what they fed their children on the way out of the fast-food place next door. She saw the same rounded shoulders, the same limp in the same age ankles, the same deep coughs, just in different coats.

Sometimes a kid stopped and pointed.

"Duckie," a little girl said, pressing sticky fingers to the glass. "Look, Mom. She has outfits."

"Come on," the mother said, not looking up.

One afternoon, a couple in matching logo jackets paused.

"That suitcase would look cute in the foyer under that mirror," the woman said. "And the duck—oh my God, she's perfect for the porch. Old-time kitsch."

The man checked the price tag, shrugged, and went inside.

A bell chimed. Hands lifted Lady off the suitcase. For a moment, she hung in the air, seeing her own reflection and the street behind it at the same time. Then the world turned toward a new place.

The perfect development

The first thing she saw was the sign.

It wasn't a hand-painted street marker like her old block. This was a stone wall with carved letters and a little waterfall, flanked by tidy shrubs planted in straight rows by people who didn't live there.

Beyond the entrance, the houses unrolled in neat loops: three- and four-bedroom boxes, each with a gable and a porch, each painted in a slightly different shade from the same four-color strip. Driveways lined up like teeth. Mailboxes matched. So did the LED porch lamps, glowing the same cold white at dusk.

Backyards were carved into rectangles by six-foot plastic fences, beige and gray and white, stretching in long unbroken lines. Here and there a play set poked up above them like a mast: tiny forts, swings, faded slides. Circles of blue and gray showed where above--ground pools sat on flattened earth. A few black trampolines huddled behind netting like caught spiders.

They set Lady on the front porch of House 12B, on a concrete step still dusted with chalk lines from where the builder had marked cuts. The blue suitcase went just inside the door, to be "sorted later."

From this new spot, Lady had a wide view.

On Sundays, the development came outside.

Men in team hats and moisture-wicking shirts washed and waxed new cars in the driveways, working in careful circles. The water ran down to the street in soapy streams. Children swung baseball bats in little bare patches of dirt, thwacking balls into practice nets that swallowed each hit with a dull pop.

Grills coughed smoke from almost every patio. The smell of meat and lighter fluid drifted over fences and across the narrow strip of new sod. Dogs in bandanas trotted at the ends of leashes, nails clicking on the walk. Some wore little raincoats or sweaters that matched their owners' shoes.

Women jogged past in matching brands, earbuds in, ponytails swinging, a layer of foundation and mascara holding steady under the sweat. A few pushed jogging strollers, babies inside, de munching crackers from crinkly bags. Neighbors paused at the corners, hands on their hips, talking about promotions, tournaments, college admissions, and sales at the warehouse club.

No one mentioned how much their chest hurt when they climbed the stairs. Not out loud.

On weekdays, the street went hollow.

The sun climbed, and garage doors yawned open just long enough for cars to nose out and head toward the freeway. By nine o'clock, Lady could see almost no one except the landscapers.

Crews of men in sun-faded shirts rolled loud mowers off trailers, marched blowers across perfect lawns, trimmed hedges into cubes and domes. Engines whined and roared and then moved on, house to house, yard to yard, leaving short green clippings on the sidewalks like confetti.

Delivery trucks replaced them: cardboard, groceries, meal kits, more cardboard. Boxes stacked on porches, then disappeared when someone slipped home for lunch or after dark. Every few weeks, a moving semi would heave its way into the subdivision, unloading another household of furniture that looked almost like the furniture already on the street.

At night, a soft rush of freeway noise floated over the roofs, a steady ocean of wheels and engines. The sky glowed faintly on the horizon, where the big stores stood, including the one everyone said was "only fifteen minutes away," as if that were a law rather than a choice.

On the sides of many houses, white pipes climbed from the foundation to the eaves, capped with little fans that hummed softly. The radon systems worked all day and all night, pulling something invisible out of the ground and sending it somewhere else, the way people sent their trash cans to the curb and their worries to the doctor's office.

From her step, Lady watched it all.

Old street, new houses

If she closed her eyes—if a plastic duck could close her eyes—the sounds and shapes from her old street still rose like heat from blacktop.

She remembered the widow's thin ankles on the porch and the way her chest rose and fell more slowly each year. The garage was packed to the ceiling with "just in case," until strangers came and hauled it all away in a weekend. Somewhere, on a block she would never see, another family now sat in that apartment, eating different food in the same stale air.

She remembered the lawn-ornament son with his perfect grass, the casino trips, the oxygen hose trailing behind his mother's chair. By now, his knees would be worse, his chest heavier. Maybe he had hung a new decoration where she once stood. Maybe another cheap bird stared at the same street, learning the same lessons too late.

She thought of the minivan family: late-night dinners in front of glowing screens, fast-food wrappers stuffed into the trash, pill bottles and inhalers multiplying on the counter. One child,d grown, is back home after college, and paying off loans. Another is still wheezing after gym class. New model van, same drive-through line.

The TV neighbor with the cat and the snacks had either moved into a smaller room with a call button and a plastic wristband or been replaced by someone else who left the screen on for company. Either way, the glow in that window would look the same from the street.

The young couple with the citrus-clean house and the dog had walked through years of chemicals and long hours into the hard light of the diagnosis they never thought would be theirs. Maybe her hair had grown back. Perhaps it hadn't. Perhaps he still scrolled on his phone in the recliner after work, telling himself they would start walking more "when things settled down."

The women with the electric car still printed signs and went to meetings, rallying for skies they rarely stood under without a phone in their hands. The high-turnover rental still burned through tenants, furniture, and promises. The dog-walkers with the candy bars were older now, their steps shorter, their leashes in new hands.

Lady had watched decades of small decisions harden into outcomes: the slow bend of spines, the quiet clogging of arteries, the way habits took root deeper than the maple's roots ever had.

Now she watched this new development, shiny and proud and already tired at the edges, and saw the same movie starting again on different screens.

Here were the Food-and-Screen caves with three flat-panel TVs and a permanent light in the pantry. Here were the Chemical Palaces, where the air smelled "clean" like a hospital every Saturday morning. Here were the overstuffed closets, the garages so full the new trucks slept on the driveway, the kids raised on sugar and screens and tight schedules.

The houses were bigger. The fences were higher. The cars were newer. The story did not care.

A small change

Not everything was the same.

Across the street, at the corner lot, a man who used to drive past in a suit had started coming out in the evenings in plain shorts and an old T-shirt. At first, he walked alone, just once around the block, phone in hand, shoulders tight.

One night, they left the phone on the porch rail.

The following week, a child joined him, helmet askew, wobbling a bike. The man jogged beside the back wheel, one hand hovering over the seat, laughing when the bike tipped and righted itself. They circled the street in wider and wider loops—past the cars, past the mailboxes, past Lady—without earbuds, without screens.

On trash day, Lady saw the man set a single bag by the curb, lighter than the two overstuffed cans he had dragged out when they first moved in. The empty snack boxes on top were fewer in number. The grill smoked less often. Sometimes, when they drove out on Saturday mornings, there were dirt bikes on a rack and backpacks in the back, mud on the tires when they returned.

It was not a miracle. He still had a car, a mortgage, and a yard the landscapers trimmed. But something in his pattern had shifted a few inches, and everything attached to it tugged along.

Lady noticed.

No one had taught her to keep track of these things. No one had set out to listen to the quiet math of everyday choices in other people's houses. She was only plastic and paint and hollow space.

But after one porch and one window and one new development, she knew this much:

Houses came and went. Lawns greened and browned, then rolled up and hauled away. People bought decorations in one decade and threw them into dumpsters in another. What lasted longest were the habits—the way hands reached for certain foods, the way feet stayed still or moved, the way eyes chose screens or sky.

The habits outlived the roofs. The habits outlived the trees. Sometimes, Lady thought, the habits outlived the people.

Watching

The wind shifted, bringing a faint tang of exhaust from the freeway and a hint of grilled meat from three houses down. Somewhere beyond the subdivision, a train horn blew. In the distance, down the main road, the light over the big-box store sign flickered on for the night shift.

A boy on a scooter shot past, one foot pumping, hair stuck to his forehead. He glanced at Lady as he went by, just long enough to bump a wheel off the curb.

"Cool duck," he muttered, and kept going.

It wasn't much. But it was more than nothing.

Lady stood on her new step, beak pointed at the street, feet bolted to her concrete base. She had watched one neighborhood grow, sag, and crack. She would watch this one, too.

She could not move. She could not speak. She could only do the one thing no one else seemed to have time for.

She would look.

If anyone, hurrying past with a leash or a latte or a sack of drive-through food, ever stopped long enough to look back, they might finally see what she had seen not just on that first block, but in the shop window and on this perfect little street. If they did, then maybe, on some future porch in some other place, a duck would spend a very long time watching something new.

Chapter Fourteen

Author's Note

This story grew out of forty-five years of walking into other people's homes. I've spent my life as a full-time home inspector, landlord, and short-term rental host, and as the author of twenty-seven books written between 2019 and 2026 about environmental health, building failures, and what our dwellings quietly do to our bodies and minds. Every porch, hallway, basement, and bedroom I've entered has been a kind of classroom. The teacher was never in the house. It was the people living inside it.

When I was younger, I rented a small place from a landlady who kept a concrete duck on the porch and changed its outfits with the seasons. Later, I lived on a street where two families, facing each other, also had a porch duck. I'd catch myself staring at those birds more than at my neighbors, watching the costumes change while the people stayed on the same treadmill. That is where Lady came from.

She's made of plastic in these pages, but the lives she watches are real composites, drawn from thousands of houses and hundreds of neighborhoods I've inspected, and from the patterns that showed up again and again in my work. Different cities, different incomes, different paint colors. The same junk food, the same blue light, the same stress, the same "someday" that rarely comes.

We pour enormous time, money, and health into things that do not love us back. Extra square footage we barely walk through. Screens that eat our evenings. Upgrades, decor, and storage units for objects we don't use. Commutes, practices, shopping trips, and scrolling sessions that leave us too tired to think. There's a brutal opportunity cost hiding in all that: years that could have gone to real rest, real movement, authentic relationships, or real curiosity about what's making us sick. Instead, we're sold a script by advertising, social media, school, and even well-meaning family that says more, newer, bigger, faster is normal and deserved. We call it lifestyle. But from the porch, it often looks more like soft, polite self-destruction.

Most of the people I've met weren't lazy, stupid, or evil. They were busy. So busy that whole decades vanished into work, errands, medication refills, streaming, and drive-through dinners. Busy enough that they never stood still long enough to see their own patterns. Lady is what happens if you force someone to stand still.

If you were bolted to a porch for twenty years and had nothing to do but watch your street, your trash, your neighbors' habits, and your own health outcomes, you might start asking uglier questions. How much of my day is actually chosen, and how much is scripted for me? What am I trading my lungs, liver, joints, and brain for, exactly? Which of my regular routines would look insane if I watched them from ten feet away for a decade?

The disturbing answer, in house after house, is that minimal changes, even when the warning signs are loud. A stroke doesn't break the TV habit. A cancer scare doesn't magically empty the pantry or the storage unit. A near-miss in the emergency room doesn't always pull people out of the drive-through line. The system we live inside is built to keep you comfortably numb and constantly occupied. That's the quiet horror this little duck book is really about.

I'm not asking you to become a lawn ornament. But I am inviting you to borrow Lady's eyes for a moment. Look at your own porch, trash, calendar, and screens the way an outsider would. Watch your street for a year, the way she has watched hers for decades. Notice what is growing and what is quietly dying in the background while you are too busy to notice. If that feels uncomfortable, good. Discomfort is the first crack in the concrete.

You just spent a whole book standing still with a duck, watching other people's lives play out. The real question now is terrifying and straightforward: what would you see—what might you finally change—if you did that with your own?

Chapter Fifteen

Further reading

Main Collection

BIAS: How Our Minds Deceive Us – 18 Ways Your Perceptions Are Skewed and How to See More Clearly

Childless Cat Lady – Movement, Dynamics, Health, and Political Influence

Don't Rent This Home, Condo, or Apartment

Empty Cradles – Declining Birth Rates Explained

Fix Your Toxic Home and Live Longer

Forever Chemicals – How PFAS Pollutes Our Blood and Lives

Make Your Home Great Again (For Homeowners and Buyers) – Expanded Tips Edition

Nuclear Extinction Event Is Killing Our Families

Pets: The Hidden Costs of Companionship

Poisoned at the Grocery Store – Why Shopping Fresh

Is Not Enough to Escape a Toxic Food Supply
Project 2025 Quick Review
Surviving Electrosmog – How to Understand and Reduce Invisible Pollution in Your Home and Life
The Sixth Extinction: Return to Earth 2225 – Dystopian fiction about how the Anunnaki return to a scarred Earth with only 500,000 people left
Heaven Is a Misfiled Ticket – A comic novel about a man who is sent to the wrong heavens by mistake
The Water You Drink May Be Killing You
No-Mow Living – The Real Hidden Costs of Grass

Forthcoming Books (2026–2027)

(Working titles; final names may change)
Pressure Canning – Safe Preservation of Food at Home
Above-Ground Gardening – Growing Food Without Digging Up Your Yard
Grow Your Own Teas – How to Harvest and Blend Them for Holistic Use
Trump's First Year – A Highly Political Review
The Duck Who Watched – A reality-fiction novel about a porch duck that quietly watches the houses across the street

Many of these longer works will also be adapted into shorter guides and papers in 2026–2027.

White Papers

Hidden Drivers of Population Decline – How Modern Health, Environmental, and Medical Risks Create Empty Cradles

Indoor Pets, Hidden Costs – Health, Housing, Money, and the Environment in Pet-Centric Living

Earth Helpers Kids' Series

PFAS KIDS – The Forever Chemical Mystery

The Great Smoke, Fire & Dust Adventure

EMF KIDS – The Secret World of Invisible Waves

Nuclear KIDS – Little Lessons from Atomic Power

Grass KIDS – Why the Lawn Isn't Always Greener

Home Safety KIDS – Smart Habits for Everyday Dangers

Lucky to Be Alive – Discover Why Every Life Is a Miracle

The Vitamin ABC's – A Healthy Kids' Guide

Eight additional Earth Helpers Kids' Series titles are planned for 2026–2027. To find any of these titles, search for "Marko Vovk" on Amazon.

Made in the USA
Monee, IL
04 November 2026

67381906R00105